D1264287

LORD NELSON

IMMORTALS OF HISTORY

LORD NELSON

By

Commander Herbert J. Gimpel,
USN (Ret.)

Franklin Watts, Inc.
575 Lexington Avenue
New York, N. Y. 10022

Front cover painting of Lord Nelson is by John Hoppner and is reproduced by the permission of National Maritime Museum, Greenwich, London.

FIRST PRINTING

Library of Congress Catalog Card Number: 66-14564
Manufactured in the United States of America

TO DON

"One of the few, the immortal names,
that were not born to die."

—Halleck

Contents

PREFACE

In the age of nuclear power, it is difficult for the reader to imagine himself on the quarterdeck of a sailing ship in Nelson's day. The agony of a skipper becalmed, or bucking against a contrary wind, belongs to navies of the past. The propellers of our powerful ships today knife through the water while the keel plows deep in any direction or speed set on the ship's bridge. At the mercy of the wind and weather, the storm-tossed sailing ships saved an empire, and helped shape the world we know.

The many quotations which enliven the pages of this book have, in some cases, been slightly changed for clarity. However, the meaning of those quotations has been carefully preserved.

A wealth of information from numerous historians and biographers must be gratefully acknowledged in the writing of this book. Among the many helpful librarians at the Library of Congress and elsewhere, for whose assistance I am much indebted, Miss Georgia Cowan and Miss Elizabeth Cole of the District of Columbia Library stand out at the top of their profession.

In searching through a vast treasure of books, periodicals, and illustrations, my wife, Ruth, spent many long hours helping with research, in addition to editing and typing the manuscript. Lord Nelson is sure to remain a prominent figure in our household.

It is hoped that through these pages, Lord Nelson will come to life, and help inspire the sea-going and landlubber alike.

Commander Herbert J. Gimpel, USN (Ret.)
Bethesda, Maryland

CHAPTER ONE

"WHAT HAS POOR HORATIO DONE?"

A small boy of twelve climbed up the ladder of a 64-gun ship-of-the-line, and stepped onto the quarter-deck. It was the first time he had ever stood on the deck of a British ship. As he looked up at the towering masts and listened to the coarse and colorful language of the seamen, he knew that he had stepped into a new world—the world of the sea and sailing ships.

Hardly noticed by the officers and men of His Majesty's Ship *Raisonnable*, Horatio Nelson looked around in wide-eyed excitement and fascinated bewilderment. Seamen hauled on lines lashed around boxes, bales, barrels, and bags, as they stowed ship's stores belowdecks in preparation for a sea voyage. Horatio's eyes danced to take in everything at once in this new world—it was his new home as well. His paternal home was now behind him—ahead lay adventures which fired the imagination of the young country boy.

Horatio was looking for his Uncle Maurice, Captain Suckling, who was the commanding officer of the ship. His uncle had launched a career for him at sea in His Majesty's Royal Navy. Horatio was a small boy in a big ship, about to sail out on the great oceans and visit strange lands beyond the seas.

Young Horatio had traveled from his home in the rectory of Burnham Thorpe, Norfolk, where his family, poor in earthly goods, led a life that was rich in religious piety. The Reverend Edmund Nelson, his father, was rector of the parish of Burnham Thorpe, a town along the North Sea coast of England. It is a remote and rural village where the north winds sweep directly across the open sea from the arctic. These chilly winter blasts added little comfort to the Nelson household, already suffering under the burden of a large family, and living on the meager pay of a country parson.

On September 29, 1758, the Nelson family was blessed with their sixth child—a frail boy whose name, Horatio, seemed rather heroic for such an unpromising-looking hero. He was called both Horace and Horatio, names originating from the distinguished family ancestry on his mother's side. Her maiden name was Catherine Suckling, a sister to Captain Maurice Suckling, and grandniece to Sir Robert Walpole, a former prime minister of Great Britain. She was also related to the famous writer, Horace Walpole.

When Horatio was only nine years old, his mother died, having had eleven children in her eighteen years of married life. Horatio loved her dearly, and carried fond memories of her throughout his later years. He had first learned his dislike for the French at his mother's knee, and she kindled the spark of glory for the British Navy that glowed so brightly in Horatio's heart. These memories served him well when he later fought the French and led his men into battle with such zeal and success.

Horatio was a small, blue-eyed boy with straw-colored hair, who looked delicate compared with some of his more robust playmates. But he more than made up for his slight build with a courageous spirit and moral strength which made him stand out from the other lads of the village.

A story is told of Horatio and his older brother starting out for school on their ponies through the deep snowdrifts of a Norfolk winter. When the drifts appeared too deep to continue, they returned to the rectory, and told their father that they could not make it to school that day.

"If that be the case," the clergyman replied, "you certainly shall not go—but make another attempt. If the road is dangerous, you may return—but remember boys, I leave it to your honor."

The two brothers set out again on their ponies, and the older brother decided to turn back several times. Each time Horatio reminded him: "Remember, it was left to our honor."

The Nelson boys made it to school that day because of the same determination Horatio was to show many times later in his illustrious naval career. Throughout his life he would consider honor above everything else, and he always responded to a difficult challenge with almost superhuman tenacity.

The death of Horatio's mother on the day after Christmas, 1767, added to the difficulty of running the large household at the Burnham Thorpe rectory. Catherine Nelson's two brothers arrived at the chilly stone rectory for their sister's funeral. They each promised to look after a nephew to ease the burden of the large, and now motherless, family. Mr. William Suckling, an official in the Customs Office, would find a position for one. Captain Maurice Suckling would provide for another in the Royal Navy.

Three of the Nelson children had died in infancy, leaving eight to be cared for. The oldest brother, Maurice, was sent at the age of fifteen to become a clerk in the Customs Office. The next in line was William, a robust and husky lad who seemed to be built for the rugged life at sea. However, this was not to be!

During the Christmas holidays of 1770, an interesting article appeared in the paper. It stated that because a war with Spain threatened over possession of the Falkland Islands, HMS *Raisonnable* was being recommissioned for possible action under the command of Captain Maurice Suckling.

Horatio coaxed his brother to write a letter to their father, who was then at Bath because of his rheumatism.

"Do, William, write to my father, and tell him that I should like to go to sea with Uncle Maurice."

Reverend Nelson wrote to Captain Suckling, who replied with astonishment at the idea of sending the frail Horatio to sea.

"What has poor Horatio done, who is so weak, that he, above all the rest should be sent to rough it out at sea? But let him come, and the first time we go into action a cannon-ball may knock off his head, and provide for him at once!"

On a chilly morning in the early spring of 1771, Horatio and his father set out for London to launch the new sailor on his career. His father, dressed in the somber cloth of the clergy, was a tall, awkward man with large, sad eyes, and a shock of white hair which fell to his shoulders. Although he was pious and dedicated, he was not too practical in worldly matters. He said good-bye to his young son at London, and sent him alone on the stagecoach for Chatham.

When Horatio arrived at Chatham, he could see the *Raisonnable* at anchor in the Medway, but no one was expecting him, and he had no way of getting out to the ship. Finally, an officer, upon hearing the name of Captain Suckling, saw to it that young Horatio was rowed out to the *Raisonnable*.

Once on the ship's deck, he learned that his Uncle Maurice was not on board. Since no one had heard about him, he wandered about, fascinated by the activity, as the crew bustled about the decks and clambered up the rigging. Horatio dodged out of the way as orders were shouted and lines were rigged to haul supplies up the side and down into the holds.

On his first day in the Navy, Horatio could look from the deck of the HMS *Raisonnable* and see the impressive HMS *Victory* where, almost thirty-five years later, he would spend his last day in His Majesty's Navy. The life of Lord Nelson is the story of what happened during those years.

CHAPTER TWO

"LET ME GET A BLOW AT THIS DEVIL"

Young Nelson learned the ship's routine in HMS *Raisonnable*, but he did not experience the blood and thunder of battle. The war with Spain over the Falkland Islands did not materialize since Spain yielded to the British demands. After about a year of service, the *Raisonnable*, along with other ships of the Royal Navy, was placed out of commission.

The Falkland Islands incident did not produce the cannon-ball to "knock off his head and provide for him at once," but it did serve to introduce Horatio to the Royal Navy. By going to sea so early, he paid the penalty of having his formal education curtailed. Thus, in spite of his brilliant mind, his letters never attained the grammatical correctness and polish of some of his fellow officers.

Although his schooling suffered, Uncle Maurice saw to it that his nephew did not lack for training as a seaman. With the *Raisonnable* out of commission, Captain Suckling suggested that young Horatio embark on a voyage in a merchant ship to learn practical seamanship. Accordingly, he put to sea in a West India trading ship whose master, John Rathbone, had served under Captain Suckling in HMS *Dreadnought*. During a year of sailing in this Caribbean merchantman, Nelson learned his marlinspike seamanship, particularly in handling the canvas aloft.

"If I did not improve my education," Nelson said, looking back at his merchant service, "I returned a practical seaman, with a horror of the Royal Navy."

The strict and harsh discipline in the British Navy of the eighteenth century was well-known, and dreaded by all seamen. Nevertheless, in July, 1772 Horatio resumed his service in His Majesty's fleet.

"It was many weeks before I got in the least reconciled to a Man-of-War," he wrote, "so deep was the prejudice rooted."

Upon leaving the *Raisonnable*, Captain Suckling was given command of HMS *Triumph*, a 74-gun ship, stationed as guardship in the Medway River. When young Nelson first went on board he served as the captain's servant.

It was fortunate for Nelson—and for Great Britain—that Horatio's Uncle Maurice took an interest in furthering his nephew's career in the Navy. Captains then were permitted to sign on a number of midshipmen, and other hands, in their own ships. In the eighteenth century, receiving patronage was almost a necessity for getting ahead in any career. Without it, talent, promise, and years of hard labor could pass unnoticed until old age overtook ambition and killed incentive.

True to his promise, Captain Suckling provided his nephew with the opportunity to develop his great abilities and to learn the art of seamanship from keel to masthead. While attached to the *Triumph*, Horatio was permitted to handle the guardship's cutter and decked longboat.

"Thus by degrees," he wrote, "I became a good pilot, for the vessels of that description, from Chatham to the Tower of London, down the Swin, and the North Foreland; and confident of myself amongst rocks and sands."

Although piloting the boats attached to the *Triumph* was a challenge for young Nelson, he did well, and advanced in boat handling and navigation. Nevertheless, he was always alert for greater adventures.

Hearing of a polar expedition, he wasted no time in volunteering for it, only to find that no boys were allowed to go. Although Nelson was not quite fifteen years old, he applied directly to Captain Skeffington Lutwidge of HMS *Carcass*. Through persuasion he eventually became the coxswain of the captain's boat, and succeeded in embarking on the polar expedition despite his youth.

The *Carcass*, with another ship, the *Racehorse*, sailed northward to the Seven Islands, and later discovered Walden Island. The ships were finally stopped by the arctic ice within ten degrees of the North Pole. As they lay gripped in the polar ice, it was feared that the ships would have to be abandoned, and all hands would have to take to small boats. Always ready to assume responsibility and to volunteer for dangerous assignments, Nelson wasted no time in asserting himself.

"When the boats were fitted out to quit the two ships blocked in the ice," he later wrote, "I exerted myself to have command of a four-oared cutter . . . with twelve men."

The ships were finally freed from the crushing pressure of the ice, and it was not necessary to abandon them. Although the expedition produced no great discoveries, it provided an incident which showed Nelson's personal courage and fearlessness—the same qualities which became so conspicuous in his later naval career.

One night during the midwatch, between midnight and four o'clock in the morning, Nelson and a young seaman decided to sneak away from the ship to hunt a polar bear. Stealing away in the brightness of the polar night, they took advantage of an oncoming, chilly fog to conceal their departure. Excited by the prospect of finding a polar bear, young Nelson led the way over the jagged ice, clutching a rusty musket in one hand.

As the fog thickened, the two lads were missed on board the ship, and Captain Lutwidge and the other officers became deeply concerned. By the time the fog lifted, after three in the morning, the two reckless hunters were seen attacking a huge bear. Nelson's musket had misfired, and he was out of ammunition. A signal was made for their return, but Nelson's companion could not persuade him to abandon the attack.

"Never mind," Nelson responded in the face of disaster, "let me get a blow at this devil with the butt-end of my musket, and we shall have him."

Nelson's shipmate, unsure of who was going to have whom, promptly retreated to the ship. When the captain saw Nelson's extreme danger, he fired one of the ship's guns, and succeeded in scaring away the snarling bear. That shot was a most important one for, without it, Nelson stood an excellent chance of never returning from the polar cruise.

Although Captain Lutwidge could not help admiring Nelson's courage, he nevertheless reprimanded him severely for taking such a reckless chance with his life. The boy never forgot that lecture. When asked why he did such a rash thing, he replied, "Sir, I wished to kill the bear, that I might carry its skin to my father." The captain was much more interested in delivering Nelson's skin whole and intact at the end of the expedition.

CHAPTER THREE

"NOTHING LESS THAN A DISTANT VOYAGE"

The enchantment of distant places was equally as alluring to young men of the eighteenth century as it is to young men of today. Young Horatio, now fifteen years old, had already been to the West Indies, the Arctic, and he had seen much of England's coastal waters. When he heard of a squadron fitting out for a cruise to the East Indies, he quickly applied to ship out with it.

"Nothing less than a distant voyage," Nelson wrote, "could in the least satisfy my desire of maritime knowledge."

In less than two weeks after he returned from the Arctic in the *Carcass*, he was signed on as one of the ship's company of the 20-gun HMS *Seahorse*. Captain George Farmer was a strict and excellent captain who could well advance Nelson's "maritime knowledge," and the *Seahorse* was most certainly bound for distant ports!

Sailing from Spithead on November 19, 1773, Horatio watched the shores of England grow smaller astern, until the land dipped under the horizon. Ahead lay the wonders of the East Indies, from the Bay of Bengal to Bombay and Basra. During this cruise, Nelson stood foretop watches and qualified as a midshipman. Under Captain Farmer's keen eye, the midshipmen were taught to take celestial sightings in order to further their ability to navigate. The captain also demanded that they keep an accurate and exemplary ship's log.

The training on board the *Seahorse* was thorough —the discipline was strict and unbending. Nelson's previous cruises had been in the merchant service, or under the fatherly tutelage of his Uncle Maurice and Captain Lutwidge. Now he was learning to stand on his own without any special consideration for his youth.

To Nelson's credit it can be said that his eagerness to learn and to excel kept him well clear of the harsh discipline on board. Others did not fare as well. The first lieutenant of the *Seahorse* was rapped with a court-martial, and various members of the crew were lashed with the cat-o'-nine-tails on at least two hundred separate floggings.

In Nelson's day, the captain of a ship could order punishment by flogging for any offense which he or his officers considered serious enough. The prisoner had to strip to the waist, and his wrists were bound and secured to a grating or to a capstan bar. After the officer read the sentence of the court-martial, he ordered the boatswain's mates to "do their duty."

The cat-o'-nine-tails then was lashed across the prisoner's bare back. After about ten lashes, the first boatswain's mate was relieved by another. The mates were drilled to apply the "cat" effectively by practicing on a cask, under the supervision of the boatswain.

One or two dozen lashes might be applied—at other times, two or three hundred might be laid on. Often the bleeding victim mercifully collapsed into an unconscious state and died. When a prisoner was "flogged around the fleet" he would be lashed, released, and rowed on to the next ship, until he had been punished on board all of the ships present.

"It generally happens," one report reads, "that nature is unable to sustain it, and the poor fellow faints and sinks under it, although every kind method is made use of to enable him to bear it, by pouring wine down his throat. The doctor will then feel his pulse, and often pronounces that the man is unable to bear more. He is then taken, most usually insensible, to what is termed the 'sick bay'; and, if he recovers, he is told he will have to receive the remainder of his punishment. When there are many ships in the fleet at the time of the court-martial, this ceremony, if the prisoner can sustain it, will last nearly half the day."

For talking back in a disrespectful way, the victim was usually gagged—his hands were bound behind him, his legs placed in irons, and an iron bar placed through his mouth, holding his jaws open.

In one ship, the HMS *Hermione*, the captain chose to flog the last man down from aloft when they were working the sails. As a result, every time the men had to scramble up into the rigging, someone was flogged. No matter how fast the men worked, someone had to be last, however fast he descended to the deck. In the rush, men were hurt, and some were killed. The outrage so infuriated the crew that they finally mutinied, and murdered the captain and his officers.

One of the common punishments given to midshipmen who did not respond smartly to orders was "mastheading." The midshipmen, unaccustomed to working aloft, were sent on a dizzying climb to the top of the mast. With the pitch and roll of the deck far below them, the long masts described crazy arcs in the sky. It took a stout heart to withstand these spine-tingling flirtations with eternity.

When Nelson became a captain, he sent his midshipmen aloft as a means of training them to overcome their fear, and often accompanied them on the climb. He also did much to remove many of the atrocious conditions under which the seamen lived.

The twentieth century reader usually envisions an old ship-of-the-line in terms of fresh ocean breezes singing through the shrouds and billowing canvas, as the ship majestically sails across the bounding blue sea. Perhaps it is fortunate that the romantic lenses of time have obscured our vision of the filth, dampness, and disease which infested the lower decks where the crew lived. The overworked, underpaid seaman who ventured a protest against these intolerable conditions might well have his complaint answered by a dozen or more lashes with the cat-o'-nine-tails.

Even the midshipmen's quarters were dark and dingy places, where rats and roaches romped freely in the eternal scramble for survival. The damp and crowded lower deck reeked heavily from the bilge, with no ventilation to carry off the stale air. The food served was disgraceful and sickening—biscuits crawling with maggots "cold to the tooth," beef so hard it could be carved like ivory, and salt pork long spoiled. The water smelled so foul it hardly could be swallowed. It was recorded that "a hot country, stinking meat, maggoty bread, noisome and poisonous scent of the bilge-water have made many a brave sailor food for crabs and sharks."

After cruising for over two years in the *Seahorse* in the extreme heat and withering climate of the Indian Ocean, the Bay of Bengal, and the Persian Gulf, Nelson finally was struck down with a malarial fever. While at Bombay in December, 1775, the ship's surgeon from the HMS *Salisbury* advised that he be sent home as his only hope of recovery. A huskier shipmate and good friend of his, Midshipman Troubridge, stayed on board the *Seahorse*, but they were to see much more of each other in their later naval service.

When Nelson eventually embarked in the HMS *Dolphin* for passage to England, he was little more than a skeleton, and partially paralyzed. While homeward bound, he knew that he was close to death, and in his feverish state he had an inspirational vision. "A sudden glow of patriotism was kindled within me," he later confided to his fellow officers. He sensed that he might one day be a great leader in naval combat, and he was determined that, "confiding in Providence, I will brave every danger."

During the six-month voyage home, around the African continent, Nelson responded to the kindness and excellent care given him by Captain Pigot. By the time he reached England's shores again in September, 1776, an unusual spirit glowed in Nelson. He was a young man of eighteen, with a gleam in his eye, and an appointment with destiny. His life, he felt, had been saved for the purpose of serving his country. Nothing would stop him from fulfilling that destiny—"for God and my country."

CHAPTER FOUR

"A BLOODY WAR AND A SICKLY SEASON"

Not long after Nelson returned to England in the *Dolphin*, he felt strong enough to go to sea again. On September 26, 1776, he received orders to the 64-gun HMS *Worcester* as acting lieutenant. During the next six months, he splendidly performed the duties of lieutenant in the Royal Navy while the *Worcester* sailed on convoy duty between England and Gibraltar.

Although he was extremely young to be entrusted with a watch in a sailing ship-of-the-line, Captain Robinson stated that he "felt as easy when Nelson was upon the deck, as any officer in the ship." By the time he left the *Worcester*, the second of April, 1777, Nelson was fully qualified to assume the duties of officer-of-the-deck, and was ordered to take his examination for lieutenant.

Dressed in his smartest uniform, and carrying his records with him, Nelson walked into a room full of strangers—the examining board of captains who were waiting for him. One of the "strangers" on the board was his Uncle Maurice, who was then the Comptroller of the Navy. He looked right through Nelson with a stony expression, as though he never had seen him before. Although slightly perplexed for a moment, the young candidate faced the board with confidence and resolution.

After he had answered all the questions promptly and well, and had passed the examination in a capital manner, Captain Suckling proudly introduced his nephew. He wanted the examining board to pass Nelson on his own merits, and not because of his influence.

"I felt convinced that he would pass a good examination," the captain said, "and you see, gentlemen, I have not been disappointed."

His uncle had provided the opportunity for Nelson to qualify for a naval career, and his nephew had come through with flying colors. This was the last time Nelson saw his uncle, for he died the following summer.

Off to sea again later in April, Nelson was fortunate in having Captain William Locker as his commanding officer in the 32-gun frigate HMS *Lowestoffe*. Locker was a fine gentleman and scholar who became Nelson's lifelong friend. There must have been something great in Nelson which Locker sensed even at the boy's early age of eighteen, for he saved all of his letters. He also arranged to have the first portrait of Nelson painted before the *Lowestoffe* departed England for the Jamaica station in the West Indies.

When the frigate arrived at Jamaica, the captain put Nelson in charge of the *Lowestoffe*'s tender, the schooner *Little Lucy*, named after Miss Lucy Locker.

Sailing in this schooner was the sort of independent duty which Nelson loved.

"I made myself a complete pilot," he wrote, "for all the passages through the Islands situated on the north side of Hispaniola (Haiti)." England was then at war with her colonies in North America, and France was soon to join the hostilities against her traditional British enemies.

Captain Locker's health failed in the summer of 1778, and Nelson was transferred to Sir Peter Parker's flagship HMS *Bristol*, as third lieutenant. He was bound to miss his good friend Locker very much. However, Admiral Parker quickly gained confidence in Nelson's abilities, and both he and Lady Parker grew very fond of him. In this way a long friendship developed again, as it had with Captain Locker. Nelson proved to be a very congenial shipmate with a cordial disposition. He was always eager to help a friend or support a superior whose loyalty was deserved.

Lieutenant Nelson also gained another lifelong admirer—Lieutenant Collingwood, who relieved him in a succession of assignments. Both were excellent officers whose promise caught the keen eye of Admiral Parker. His decisions in promoting them were guided by sound judgment, as their brilliant careers proved. Collingwood relieved Nelson in the *Lowestoffe*, *Bristol*, the brig *Badger*, and the frigate *Hinchinbrooke*. Many years later, Collingwood succeeded to Nelson's fleet command after the Battle of Trafalgar.

Aboard the *Bristol*, Nelson quickly advanced from third lieutenant to first lieutenant, as sickness took its toll of officers above him. There was wry humor in the old toast: "A bloody war and a sickly season." Both brought about rapid promotions! The "sickly season" was not helped by the withering heat in the poorly ventilated sailing ships, which baked in the tropical sun.

By December of 1778, Nelson was promoted to Commander, and assigned to the brig HMS *Badger*. His assignment was to protect the Mosquito Coast along Central America "from the depredations of American privateers." This pestilential area included what is now the southern part of Mexico, Guatemala, Honduras, Nicaragua, Costa Rica, and Panama.

When a cannon-ball killed the captain of the frigate *Hinchinbrooke*, Admiral Parker chose Nelson to command her. He was now a post captain, and would be promoted to captain upon approval of the British Admiralty. Since ships of over twenty guns rated a captain in command, Nelson entered the list of Navy captains before his twenty-first birthday. Promotion from then on was automatic, according to seniority on the list. Nelson was one of the youngest captains in the Royal Navy—and he was later to become the youngest admiral.

During the month of June, 1779, Nelson assumed command of the 32-gun *Hinchinbrooke*, and for the next several months was engaged in defending Jamaica from the French. In the meantime, Spain joined the war against England. Thus, the area known as the Mosquito Coast of Central America became a hostile one.

In January, 1780, General Dalling of Jamaica conceived the idea of an expedition to seize Fort San Juan, located at the head of the San Juan River. Lake Nicaragua could then be controlled, along with the trade and commerce over the isthmus of Central America. Under Captain Polson, five hundred troops were ordered to advance up the river and take the fort guarding Lake Nicaragua.

Nelson's orders were to transport the troops to the harbor where the San Juan River spills into the Caribbean. Once the military force had landed, his part of the mission was accomplished. However, Nelson was never one to stand idly by while others fought.

Leaving the ship, he took forty-seven seamen and marines with him, and a few of the Mosquito Indians who helped them force their way upstream over rocks and sand. (Since the expedition was sent at the wrong time of the year, the river in April was hardly a creek in some places.) The difficulties only made Nelson more anxious to pitch in, and go up the river with the troops.

The backbreaking work of hauling boats, supplies, guns and ammunition up the tropical riverbed was hard enough for healthy men. However, the combination of climate and disease had left few who were not sick. Along the river were poisonous marshes with swarms of mosquitoes, insects, snakes, rotting vegetation wet from the humidity, and dripping foliage so thick it blotted out the sun. When the sun did shine through, the scorching heat blistered the skin. By contrast, the chilling fog of night loaded the lungs with damp, heavy air. And, over all the toil and discomfort, hovered the threat of yellow fever.

Yet Nelson could write of this situation, "I know it is my disposition that difficulties and dangers do but increase my desire of attempting them."

Nelson personally led the attack on an outpost of the Fort, located 59 miles up the river. Reaching a good spot to attack, he leaped out of the boat, and landed heavily in the muck along the riverbank. His shoes stuck fast in the mud, but he charged ahead barefooted, brandishing his sword at the head of a band of his loyal seamen. The defenders were so surprised that he took the outpost by storming it! In his nautical manner, Nelson described how he "boarded an outpost of the enemy."

When they reached Fort San Juan, about 100 miles up the river, Nelson was in favor of taking the Fort by the same method, but Captain Polson and Lieutenant Despard favored a formal siege. Since he could not persuade the military officers, he joined them in fighting their way.

"I want words to express the obligations I owe to Captain Nelson," Polson later wrote. "He was the first on every service, whether by day or night. There was not a gun fired but was pointed by him, or by Despard."

Nelson could not stay until the end of the expedition, although the hardest part of the struggle was over. He was ordered to return to take command of HMS *Janus*, a fine ship of forty-four guns. However, this was not to be, for Nelson finally collapsed from the fever of the tropical jungle.

When he returned to Jamaica to command the *Janus*, he was so sick that he was carried ashore on his cot. His brave crew of the *Hinchinbrooke* were also ravaged by yellow fever—of the 200 men in the ship, 145 were buried. The ship's doctor later reported that "very few, not more than ten, survived of that ship's crew."

Nelson was taken to the home of Admiral Parker,

where Lady Parker cared for him as if he were her own son. His health did not improve in the tropical climate and, more dead than alive, he was finally shipped home in HMS *Lion*. The captain, the Honorable William Cornwallis, was acknowledged by Nelson as the one "whose care and attention saved my life."

Arriving in England in the fall of 1780, Nelson went to Bath for the winter to recover. In a letter to his brother in May of the following year, he wrote: "I have entirely lost the use of my left arm, and very near of my left thigh."

The admirable combination of a courageous fighter with a tender heart was always evident in Nelson. He asked his brother not to mention his disabilities to his father, "for I know it will make him very uneasy, and can do no good."

Yet his recent illness seemed to have little effect on Nelson's dauntless spirit. He was still convalescing when he asked again for active duty. So far, he had survived "a bloody war and a sickly season."

CHAPTER FIVE

"LOVE AND HONOR"

The HMS *Albemarle*, which had been captured from the French, was a 28-gun frigate. She was, in Nelson's words, a "poor sailer," and hard to handle—it seemed as though the French had known that she would fall to the enemy! However, undismayed by the ship's failings, Nelson was delighted to have an active command again.

Nelson placed the *Albemarle* in commission in August of 1781—the first ship he had assumed command of in a British port. The ship's bottom had been newly sheathed with copper, and he was given his choice of officers. Captain Nelson, not yet twenty-three years old, was elated over his ship and her complement.

"I have an exceedingly good ship's company," he wrote. "Not a man or officer in her I would wish to change."

Looking forward to the prospect of another distant voyage, he was disappointed to find out that he was assigned to convoy duty in the Baltic Sea. This was hardly good duty for one whose health had been undermined by tropical fever.

"It would almost be supposed, to try my constitution," Nelson wrote. "I was kept the whole winter in the North Sea."

In October, at sea in the *Albemarle*, he was in charge of a large and important convoy of ships, sailing in company with the HMS *Argo* and the HMS *Enterprise*. The bone-chilling winds that whipped across the North Sea and tossed the ships about was only one unpleasant feature of this cruise. The merchant ships being escorted "behaved as all convoys that I ever saw did, shamefully ill; parting company every day."

Back in English waters again, the *Albemarle* anchored in the Downs, where the wintry gales buffeted the ships as they strained at their anchors. During a heavy gale in January, 1782, a large East India merchantman dragged her anchor and crashed into the *Albemarle*. Repairing the ship at Portsmouth took several months, and then she was sent to Cork, Ireland. From there she set sail in April, across the Atlantic, escorting a convoy bound for Quebec. The thirty ships in the convoy reached Newfoundland by the end of May, and sailed into Quebec by the first of July.

This was Nelson's initial visit to North America, but he saw little of Quebec on his first cruise up the St. Lawrence River. In three days he was underway again, to patrol for two months around the Cape Cod Bay area, where he succeeded in destroying several enemy ships. England was fighting the American Colonies in their War for Independence, and France had seized the opportunity to join against England.

During the middle of July, the *Albemarle* captured an American fishing schooner from Cape Cod. Since

Nelson was unfamiliar with the coastal waters of the area, he had the master of the schooner, Nathaniel Carver, brought on board as a pilot. He proved such a great help that Nelson returned his ship.

"You have rendered us, Sir, a very useful service, and it is not the custom of English seamen to be ungrateful. In the name therefore, and with the approbation of the officers of this ship, I return your schooner, and with it this certificate of your good conduct. Farewell! and may God bless you."

Nelson's consideration paid an unexpected dividend! Months later, when the crew of the *Albemarle* came down with scurvy, Carver took considerable risk in taking several crates of fowl, four sheep, and fresh vegetables out to the British ship. It was with great difficulty that Nelson persuaded Carver to accept payment for his trouble and expense.

Sailing near Boston Harbor on August 14, the fog suddenly lifted, revealing three French ships-of-the-line and a frigate. They were within gunshot of the *Albemarle*! The Frenchmen had come out of the harbor, and were sailing in hot pursuit after Nelson's single frigate. Nelson sailed into the shoals where the large French ships could not follow. His earlier piloting experience in coastal waters proved invaluable.

The French frigate *Iris* boldly advanced into the shoals, hoping to open fire and capture Nelson's ship. However, when Nelson saw that the big men-of-war were beyond gun range, he hove to in order to give battle. The *Iris*, finding herself evenly matched and unsupported by her ships-of-the-line, hauled off and went on her way.

While cruising across the Atlantic and patrolling

along the American coast, food supplies aboard the *Albemarle* grew scarce, and the crew was suffering from scurvy. In September, Nelson wrote: "For eight weeks, myself and all the officers lived upon salt beef; nor had the ship's company had a fresh meal since the 7th of April."

They returned to Quebec during the middle of September to rest, recuperate, and reprovision. The fall of the year, and the invigorating climate, moved Nelson to write: "Health, that greatest of blessings, is what I never truly enjoyed until I saw Fair Canada. The change it has wrought, I am convinced, is truly wonderful."

Nelson enjoyed good health, and also happiness, when he met Mary Simpson, an attractive Canadian girl. Although he fell very much in love, a good friend persuaded him not to marry her. There must have been a strong tug at Nelson's heart when the *Albemarle* sailed from Quebec, never to return again.

In November, the *Albemarle* dropped anchor at New York, off Sandy Hook, near the battle-scarred ships of Lord Hood's squadron. They had recently been engaged with the French Fleet, and were soon to return to the West Indies. After arriving, Nelson visited Lord Hood's flagship, HMS *Barfleur*, to pay his respects. Young Prince William Henry was on deck as midshipman of the watch, and to him we owe a colorful description of Nelson.

"Captain Nelson, of the *Albemarle*, came in his barge alongside, who appeared to be the merest boy of a Captain I ever beheld, and his dress was worthy of attention. He had on his full, laced uniform; his lank unpowdered hair was tied in a stiff Hessian tail, of an extraordinary length. The old-fashioned flaps of his waistcoat added to the general quaintness of his figure.

"There was something irresistibly pleasing in his address and conversation; and an enthusiasm, when speaking on professional subjects, that showed he was no common being. I found him warmly attached to my Father (the King), and singularly humane.

"He had the honor of the King's service, and the independence of the British Navy, particularly at heart. His mind glowed with this idea as much when he was simply captain of the *Albemarle*, as when he was afterwards decorated with so much well-earned distinction."

The squadron operating along the coast of North America had an excellent station for winning prize money by capturing enemy ships. Lord Hood, therefore, was astonished when he heard Nelson ask to leave with his squadron for the West Indies.

"Ah, but the West Indies is the station for honor," Nelson replied.

In December, Nelson was granted his request to go to the West Indies. However, the war was drawing to an end, and by the time he arrived, there was little honor to be gained.

When Great Britain made peace with Spain and America, the *Albemarle* was ordered home. She arrived at Spithead in June 1783. The ship's company was "paid off" in July, and the frigate was placed out of service.

The crew told Nelson that if he were to be given another command, they would like to ship out with him again. In those days of horrible life at sea, this was a very unusual gesture. Even before Nelson became famous, his men thought highly of him. He was always most considerate of his "fine fellows," and they responded with diligence and loyalty.

During the autumn of 1783, Nelson took advantage of peace between England and France, and made a trip across the Channel to learn French. While his vacation did not produce fluency in the French language, it did provide a romance.

While staying at St. Omer, he fell in love with the daughter of an English clergyman, a Miss Andrews. Having little money to support a young wife, he wrote to his uncle, William Suckling, for an advance. It was promptly granted. The young lady, however, had other plans, and Nelson returned to England where he immediately applied for another ship.

Obtaining command of a ship in peacetime was not easy, but in March of 1784 Nelson was assigned to the 28-gun frigate HMS *Boreas*. In May he sailed for the West Indies, where Sir Richard Hughes was the Admiral in command. Much to his surprise, Nelson found that he was to provide passage for Lady Hughes and her daughter to the West Indies, at his own expense! This put a large dent in Nelson's already meager funds, since he had been living on half pay for many months before sailing. For Nelson, it was little compensation listening to Lady Hughes's constant chatter, and her daughter was apparently not gifted with the charms of Miss Andrews.

Lady Hughes was very impressed with the great attention Nelson paid to the thirty midshipmen in the *Boreas*, whom he called "his children."

"The timid he never rebuked," she wrote, "but always wished to show them he desired nothing of them that he would not instantly do himself. I have known him to say, 'Well, Sir, I am going on a race to the masthead, and beg I may meet you there.' No denial could be given to such a wish, and the poor fellow instantly began his climb. When they met at the top, he began instantly speaking in the most cheerful manner, and saying how much a person was to be pitied who could fancy there was any danger, or even anything disagreeable in the attempt. How wise and kind was such a proceeding!

"In like manner, he went every day into the School Room, and saw them do their nautical business. At twelve o'clock he was first on deck with his quadrant. No one there could be behindhand in their business when their Captain set them so good an example.

"The day we landed at Barbados, we were to dine at the Governor's. Our dear Captain said, 'You must permit me, Lady Hughes, to carry one of my Aide-de-Camps with me.' When he presented him to the Governor he said, 'Your Excellency must excuse me for bringing one of my midshipmen, as I make it a rule to introduce them to all the good company I can.' This kindness and attention made the young people adore him."

Having delivered his "cargo" at the end of June to Sir Richard Hughes at Barbados, Nelson was not overly impressed with the undecisive Commander-in-chief. Sir Richard's appearance was not enhanced by the loss of one eye in his youth, while engaging a cockroach with a tablefork! Nelson, not yet twenty-six, was now second in command—a result of his early promotion to Captain. Differences in opinion were soon to arise between Nelson and his new Admiral.

The American colonies had won their independence, and were no longer under the British flag. As a result, trade relations with the British West Indies changed. The Navigation Act prohibited trade between foreign countries and the British colonies. Britain's military and economic strength depended upon the enforcement of this Act. However, for reasons of profit, the law was ignored. No one seemed to pay the least bit of attention to the illegal trade until Nelson came upon the scene.

The Governor of Jamaica had formally authorized free trade with the American ships. Even the customs officials were in on the illegal profits, and Sir Richard Hughes seemed unconcerned.

In spite of his youth, Nelson decided to enforce the law. This upset many plans of the local planters and merchants to make a corrupt profit. An uproar resulted when Nelson, together with his officers from the *Boreas*, boarded, inspected, and stopped the illegal trading ships from entering port. Admiral Hughes at first had agreed to support Nelson in enforcing the law, but when confronted by the angry traders, he reversed his policy. Nelson was ordered to stop his interference.

During a staff conference between the ships' captains and the Admiral's staff in November, 1784, orders were issued for winter operations. Since no mention was made of the Navigation Act, Nelson, backed by his friend Captain Collingwood, urged the enforcement of the laws.

At first, Admiral Hughes expressed ignorance of

the Navigation Act! However, he finally gave an order to enforce it. Later he weakened again, and instructed that the foreign ships should only be inspected, and reports made to the civil authorities. They would then approve the entry of the merchant ships into port.

As for Nelson, he considered that he was being instructed to do something illegal. He knew he was right, and would not give an inch—not even to his Commander-in-chief. Nor would he back down when General Shirley, the Governor of St. Kitts, remarked to him: "Old generals are not in the habit of taking advice from young captains."

"I have the honor, sir, of being as old as the Prime Minister of England," Nelson replied, "and I think myself capable of commanding one of His Majesty's ships as that Minister is of governing the State."

As a result of his policy of considering honor above profit, Nelson had to remain on board the *Boreas* to escape the court summons being issued by the many profiteers who tried to stop him. The young captain's interference was downright unprofitable to them, and their anger mounted with their financial losses. Admiral Hughes did absolutely nothing to assist Nelson, and in fact warned him that he might "get himself into a scrape."

Finally, a letter arrived from the King, stating that Nelson's position would be defended by the Crown lawyers. Then another most amazing letter arrived from the Secretary of the Treasury, through the Admiralty, complimenting Admiral Hughes: "The commander-in-chief of the Leeward Islands, and officers under him, have shown a very commendable zeal, in endeavoring to put a stop to the very illicit practices which were carrying on in the islands, in open violation of the law, to the great detriment of the navigation and trade of His Majesty's dominions."

Thus Nelson's struggle with his senior commander, Sir Richard Hughes, had come to an end. Admiral Hughes apparently never did bother to correct this miscarriage of justice, and accepted for himself undue credit for the honorable performance of duty which he had lately opposed. Nelson was to see more of this sort of injustice later in his career.

Somehow, during all this legal wrangling, Nelson met the lady who was to become his wife. She was a widow named Fanny Nisbet, who had a six-year-old son, Josiah. Actually the "love affair" seemed more a matter of esteem and respect, than the rapture he had felt for Miss Andrews. However, the marriage ceremony, which took place on March 11, 1787, at Nevis, had a touch of glamour. Prince William Henry, then Captain of the *Pegasus*, gave the bride away.

The *Boreas* sailed for England in June, and dropped anchor at Spithead on the fourth of July. Nelson's bride, Fanny, followed a few months later aboard a merchant ship. Nelson's duty in the *Boreas* ended on November 30, with many threats of legal action from the West Indies traders still pending. These lawsuits took years to settle.

Nelson found it impossible to get command of another ship in peacetime. For the next five years, he lived ashore at Burnham Thorpe on half pay, with a new family to support. These were not the happiest years of his life—"love and honor" seemed to have eluded him.

CHAPTER SIX

"THE *AGAMEMNON* SAILS ADMIRABLY"

While Captain Nelson was still living peacefully with his wife at the rectory in Burnham Thorpe, the rumble of a great political storm was causing much anxiety in the courts of Europe. At the beginning of 1793, uncontrolled mobs created terror in the streets of Paris. The guillotine became a symbol of the French Revolution, as blood ran and heads rolled.

In January, 1793, Nelson's frequent requests to the Admiralty for command of a ship finally brought results. Lord Chatham, the First Lord of the Admiralty, apologized for the years of inactivity and offered Nelson a 74-gun ship as soon as one became available.

Shortly thereafter, news was received that the terrorists had beheaded the King of France, Louis XVI, and the French Ambassador was ordered to leave England. England had no choice but to fight for her empire.

Across the sea, George Washington, then serving his first term as President of the United States, had a great new country to shape and guide. The French wanted America to join in the war against England. However, the President wisely chose to maintain a strict nonpartisan attitude, and unflinchingly kept the United States "out of foreign entanglements."

Periodically the world seems destined to suffer the scourge of a skilled and successful tyrant. The twentieth century has had its Hitler, Stalin, Mussolini, and other infamous leaders. One such person during Nelson's time was Napoleon Bonaparte—a product of the boiling pot of the French Revolution.

The scarlet flow of blood from the murders of the Revolution had left the French Government in a chaotic state, and absolute power soon fell into the grasping clutches of the ambitious young general, Napoleon Bonaparte. Bonaparte was not content with administering internal affairs, and building world trade—instead, he proceeded to crush, plunder, or intimidate Spain, Italy, Germany, Austria, and the small countries of the Mediterranean.

Across the English Channel lay the apple of Napoleon's eye—England. His plans to invade the country by bloody conquest were never abandoned. They simply ran into persistent misfortune. And that misfortune was always the same—the British Navy.

Impatient to command a ship-of-the-line, Nelson did not wait for a 74-gun ship, but accepted orders to the 64-gun HMS *Agamemnon* on January 30. Two days later, the Republic of France declared war on Great Britain and Holland. From the quiet parsonage at Burnham Thorpe, Nelson emerged as the grand champion of Britain's domination of the seas. He crushed the French ambitions at sea, and helped save

Great Britain, as well as the rest of Europe, from Napoleon's greedy aggression.

Captain Nelson, then thirty-four years old, joined his ship on February 7. Tagging along was a thirteen-year-old boy, his stepson Josiah Nisbet, who was signed on in the *Agamemnon* as a midshipman.

Also on board were a number of volunteers from Nelson's own county of Norfolk—good, stout-hearted fellows, considered by their captain to be worth two of any other. As the *Agamemnon* sailed away with Nelson's handpicked crew, these men were certain to become an outstanding crew under their captain's inspiring influence.

"Nobody can be ill with my ship's company," Nelson wrote, "they are so fine a set."

Nelson also had his choice of fleets in which to serve. It was not a difficult decision—the Mediterranean Fleet, under Lord Hood, he felt was by far the best. He had a good ship under his feet, and a "fast sailer" in a sea chase. As captain of a good ship and crew, Nelson was back in his own element. He was glowing with enthusiasm, and anxious to meet the enemy for "the *Agamemnon* sails admirably. We think better than any ship in the fleet."

The ship sailed for the Mediterranean with four other ships-of-the-line, under Admiral Hotham. They joined Lord Hood's main fleet off the Scilly Islands on May 23. Their orders were to blockade Toulon—a duty which was to close one of the main French ports of trade. Nelson heard that the French were preheating, and using "red-hot" shot in their cannon.

"We must take care to get so close," he remarked, "that their red shots may go through both sides. Then it will not matter whether they are hot or cold!"

Had Nelson not been such an illustrious figure in battle, he might have made his niche in history in a different way. He was ahead of the times, with advanced ideas concerning health and morale. He insisted that the crew's living quarters be ventilated, and that stoves be used to dry the soggy beams and compartments belowdecks. Furthermore, Nelson took a personal interest in ordering food supplies for his crew. He also encouraged music and entertainment when possible to boost their morale during the monotony of endless days at sea. In short, Nelson believed in taking his "brave fellows" into battle in good health, and in a sound ship.

While blockading Toulon, Lord Hood was in touch with a French Royalist group who was not in sympathy with the bloody affairs going on in Paris. The group was hoping the British would occupy Toulon, and hold it against Napoleon's forces when they swept down into southern France. For this mission, Lord Hood needed troops.

Nelson was ordered to sail to Naples with dispatches requesting men and supplies. The *Agamemnon* arrived off Naples on September 11, but it was too late to enter port that day.

In a letter to his wife Nelson wrote:

"My dear Fanny: If Parliament does not grant something to this Fleet, our Jacks will grumble; for here there is no prize money to soften their hardships, all we get is honour and salt beef. My poor fellows have not had a morsel of fresh meat or vegetables for near 19 weeks, and in that time I have had my foot twice on shore at Cádiz.

"We are absolutely getting sick from fatigue. No Fleet, I am certain, ever served their country with greater zeal than this has done, from the Admiral to the lowest sailor.

"We are now in sight of Mount Vesuvius which shows a fine light to us in Naples Bay where we are lying-to for the night, and hope to anchor early to-morrow."

The following day Nelson sailed into port. For the first time he met many of the people who were later to play such an important part in his life—Sir William Hamilton, the British Ambassador, and Lady Hamilton; King Ferdinand and Queen Carolina of Naples, and members of the Court. His first visit to Naples lasted only four days.

We will never know whether or not Nelson fell in love with Lady Hamilton at first sight. She was a charming, blue-eyed beauty of twenty-six, and he described her as "wonderfully kind and good to Josiah. She is a young woman of amiable manners, who does honour to the station to which she is raised."

Hearing a report that a number of French ships were sailing up the coast of Italy, Nelson cancelled a reception on board for the King of Naples, and weighed anchor in two hours. As he sailed out of the harbor unsupported, he noticed seven Neapolitan men-of-war and a Spanish frigate of forty guns, all of them "otherwise employed." For nine days he searched in vain for the French ships before sailing to Leghorn "absolutely to save my poor fellows." His ship had been underway almost constantly for five months.

By the fifth of October, the *Agamemnon* had rejoined the fleet at Toulon. Four thousand Neapolitan troops had already disembarked. Lord Hood realized, more than ever, that in Nelson he had a man of unusual abilities. In diplomacy as well as in combat he acted with sound judgment and authority.

In two weeks, the sails of the *Agamemnon* were hoisted and she set course for Cagliari, a port at the south end of Sardinia. Here Nelson was to join the three ships of Commodore Linzee's squadron. Their mission was to persuade the Bey of Tunis to discontinue his favoritism toward the French. The highlight of this cruise occurred before the ship reached Cagliari.

While sailing off the coast of Sardinia on October 22, the sails of five French ships were sighted, and promptly pursued by the *Agamemnon.* The squadron included three French frigates, one of them, the *Melpomene*, carrying forty guns. Nelson's ship was shorthanded, having sent men ashore while at Toulon. In spite of this, Nelson sailed into the French formation with guns blazing.

After four hours of battle, the return fire from the French ships cut up the masts and rigging of the *Agamemnon* so badly that she was unable to continue fighting. As for the French ships, they had taken enough punishment for one day, and departed for the port of Calvi. The *Melpomene* arrived there barely able to stay afloat, only to be captured later by the British.

The battered *Agamemnon* sailed into Cagliari, where Commodore Linzee awaited his arrival. The anchor had hardly splashed over the side when Linzee asked Nelson if he were ready to sail immediately on the operation to Tunis.

"I would never say *Agamemnon* was ever unable

to go in search of the enemy," Nelson wrote. "We worked all night repairing our masts and yards, stopping shot holes, mending sails, and splicing our rigging."

Linzee's "operation" with the Bey of Tunis, during the first week of November, amounted to little more than a "damn'd palaver," according to Nelson. He was glad to be free of Linzee's command, and continued blockading duty off Genoa at the end of November. It was here that Nelson first heard of the disastrous rout of the troops at Toulon.

The inadequate British, Neapolitan, and Royalist French forces defending Toulon had little chance against the artillery of Napoleon and troops of the Republican French revolutionists. Cannon-balls crashed into the crowds of fleeing citizens, smashed houses, and set fires. The crackle of flames burned the homes of the families of Toulon while the streets, littered with the dead, ran red with blood.

The roar of Napoleon's guns triggered the retreat of the Neapolitan troops. They raced in panic-stricken flight—some of them leaping into the sea.

Lord Hood succeeded in evacuating many of the desperate citizens in his ships. When he left, he managed to sail some of the French ships out of port so that they would not fall into the hands of the Republican forces. Other ships were set on fire and left burning at anchor. By December 19, Toulon was completely in the hands of the revolutionary forces—including charred buildings, dead bodies, and wailing children.

The *Agamemnon* was loading supplies at Leghorn when some of the fugitives from Toulon arrived. Nelson wrote of the pitiful scene: "Fathers are here without families, and families without fathers, the pictures of horror and despair. My mind is deeply impressed with grief. Each teller makes the scene more horrible."

With Toulon taken by the enemy, Lord Hood needed a new base for his fleet. The Island of Corsica seemed to answer his needs—it was centrally located to the French and Italian coasts. However, at Corsica, French troops still occupied the vital ports of Bastia and Calvi.

In February, 1794, San Fiorenzo Bay was used for the British fleet anchorage. Nelson was sent from there with a detachment of frigates to blockade Bastia, on the northeast coast of Corsica. During the blockade, eight thousand enemy troops embarked at Nice to reinforce the French fort at Bastia. However, Nelson's blockade was so tight that "not a boat got in, nor a soldier landed."

Not long after arriving, Nelson urged Lord Hood to permit him to lay siege to Bastia, with the cooperation of the army. But army-navy cooperation was then very poor, and General Dundas was dead set against the idea. Nevertheless, Nelson bombarded the Fort of Bastia, which was located high up on the cliffs. He battered the fort at close range with the guns of the *Agamemnon* and his frigates.

General Dundas finally marched his troops overland from San Fiorenzo. While the bombardment from the sea was thundering against the fort, the British army troops could be seen arriving on the hills behind Bastia. Nelson was elated to see them arrive. However, the General went no farther with his troops! To Nelson's dismay, the British army forces disappeared—General Dundas declared the task was impossible with the 1,400 troops he had.

In the meantime, Nelson kept the fort in a constant state of alarm by bombardment and reconnoitering the approaches to the fort. By March, his crew and supplies were both exhausted.

"We are really without firing, wine, beef, pork, flour, and almost without water," Nelson wrote to Lord Hood. "Not a rope, canvas, twine, or nail in the ship. The ship is so light she cannot hold her side to the wind. We are certainly in a bad plight at present. Not a man has slept dry for many months.

"Yet if your Lordship wishes me to remain off Bastia, I can, by going to Port Ferrajo, get water and stores. Twenty-four hours in Leghorn will give us provisions. Our refitting, which will take some time, can be put off a little. My wish is to be present at the attack of Bastia."

In April, Nelson was put in command ashore to take Bastia—without the army. He set out to accomplish what General Dundas declared impossible, with the army and the navy. His seamen and marines dragged the heavy guns up the steep slopes, and exchanged lively fire with the French.

"It is very hard service for my poor seamen, dragging guns up such heights as are scarcely credible," he wrote.

Nelson was always at the front, spurring his men on and directing gun emplacements. During the heat of battle, he received a painful gash across his back. The defenses proved to be twice as strong as Nelson had thought, but he felt that he would "rather be beaten than not make the attack."

Guns can only do so much—the strong fortifications at Bastia were very stubborn. However, Nelson had a strong ally—hunger. His blockade had been so tight that no supplies had reached the French troops. By the nineteenth of May, flags of truce fluttered from the walls of Bastia. On the twenty-second, the French colors were struck, and the British took over.

"The more we see of this place, the more we are astonished at their giving up," Nelson observed, after the victory. "Forty-five-hundred men have laid down their arms to under twelve-hundred troops and seamen. Perseverance, unanimity, and gallantry can accomplish almost incredible things."

Although Nelson had been the inspiration, and the sustaining force of the action at Bastia, he was not given the credit he so richly deserved in Lord Hood's official report. It merely mentioned that Nelson had command of the ship's landing guns and supplies. Astonishingly, Captain Hunt was credited as the driving force in commanding the batteries. Of this Nelson wrote: "Captain Hunt is a young man who never was on a battery, or ever rendered any service during the siege. I am not a little vexed, but shall not quarrel." Actually, Lord Hood was doing Captain Hunt a favor since he had recently lost his ship, and needed the credit more than Nelson did.

"Corsica, in respect to prizes, produces nothing but honour," he wrote to Fanny. "Had I attended less than I have done to the service of My Country, I might have made some money too. However, I trust my name will stand on record when the money-makers will be forgot."

At the end of May, the *Agamemnon* was already taking on ammunition for the siege of Calvi. With

Bastia taken, only Calvi remained as a French stronghold. A walled town on the northwest coast of Corsica, Calvi is situated on a high promontory of land, with deep ravines running down the sides. The star-shaped fort protecting the town was located on the west side of a deep, three-mile-wide gulf. The attackers decided it was a poor place to land the guns and ammunition—directly under the fort—with no beachhead for a safe landing.

General Charles Stuart arrived to command the army troops, and he was much more eager to get on with the business than General Dundas had been. Stuart may have been sensitive about Nelson's victory, without the army, at Bastia. However, they cooperated well together.

Porto Agro, about three miles from Calvi, was selected as the landing spot. Here the British landed supplies and disembarked troops on June 18. Once again, the sailors skillfully used their nautical knowledge of ropes and tackles in hauling the guns and ammunition up the steep slopes, as they had done at Bastia.

"Dragging cannon up steep mountains, and carrying shot and shells has been our constant employment," he wrote to Fanny, from the encampment near Calvi. "That we shall take Calvi in due time I have no manner of doubt."

By July 3, after many grueling days, the long guns, howitzers, and mortars were in position. By then, malaria had put many of the men out of action. Captain Hallowell, who was temporarily without a ship to command, and Nelson took turns taking charge of six of the batteries.

At daybreak on July 12, a heavy barrage opened up which Nelson said, "seldom missed our battery." As the shot crashed around him, one landed directly in front of Nelson.

"A shot having hit our battery, the splinters and stones from it struck me with great violence in the face and breast," he wrote home to Fanny. "Although the blow was so severe as to occasion a great flow of blood from my head, yet I most fortunately escaped, having only my right eye nearly deprived of its sight. It is so far recovered as for me to be able to distinguish light from darkness. As to all purposes of use, it is gone. However, the blemish is nothing; not to be perceived, unless told."

His injuries kept Nelson away from duty only one day—he was back again the next day at his batteries!

After five weeks of heavy fighting, the French forces at Calvi finally surrendered on August 10. The British and French suffered great losses from injury and sickness.

"We have upwards of one thousand sick out of two thousand, and the others not much better than so many phantoms," Nelson wrote. "We have lost many men from the climate—very few from the enemy. My ship's company are all worn out, as is this whole army."

Nelson's men were glad to return to the *Agamemnon*—they had had enough of the malaria-ridden coast. One hundred and fifty of his crew were confined to their beds.

When the *Agamemnon* arrived at Leghorn in mid-August, the fleet doctor examined the crew. He was shocked by their miserable health, and declared them unfit to serve. To Fanny, Nelson wrote, "Since the ship has been in commission, this will be the first resting-time we have had."

As for the proud sailing ship, she was in as poor a condition as her crew, and remained at Leghorn for extensive repairs. Inactivity was never to Nelson's liking, and he was afraid the French Fleet might come out of the harbor at Toulon while the *Agamemnon* was still dismantled. He did not want to miss a chance of action with the French Fleet.

"He has ever showed himself as great a despiser of riches as he is a lover of glory," Admiral Radstock wrote of Nelson. "I am fully convinced in my own mind that he would sooner defeat the French fleet than capture fifty galleons."

Nelson was again to find that honors due him were given to others. General Stuart did not mention Nelson in his report—he was not even listed among those wounded! Fame and fortune had again eluded him.

All Corsica had now fallen to the British. Thanks to Nelson's courage and persistence, the seemingly impossible had been done. Lord Hood was raised in the peerage from baron to viscount. Nelson received a cut across the back, and lost his right eye!

CHAPTER SEVEN

"TIGER ON A LEASH"

Captain Horatio Nelson was at Leghorn refitting the battered *Agamemnon* when Lord Hood returned to England. The seventy-year-old Admiral had always been an outspoken man. When he asked Lord Spencer, the First Lord of the Admiralty, for reinforcements and better fleet support to fight the French, his manner was so blunt and tactless, that he was permanently relieved of his command in the Mediterranean. Nelson was shocked to hear of losing his Commander-in-chief.

Lord Hood's second in command, Lord Hotham, then became Commander-in-chief. It was not long before that officer's weak, indecisive nature clashed with Nelson's gallant spirit.

Admiral Hotham had been in charge of the close-in blockade of Toulon during the siege of Calvi. When he received word that the French Fleet was coming out of port, he sailed his ships immediately to Calvi, thinking the French Fleet superior in numbers. Later the British learned that the French ships were equal in number, and not as well seasoned. Hotham had thrown away his first chance to defeat the French before they returned to port. It would not be as easy to "play it safe" after Nelson's ship joined him.

The *Agamemnon* was again ready for sea in December, 1794—when the worst winter gales were blowing. The severe winter storms arrived with a vengeance, as *Agamemnon* joined Hotham's fleet in January.

In March, word was received from the lookout frigates that the French had put to sea from Toulon, with fifteen ships-of-the-line. The next day Hotham's fleet sailed in pursuit from Leghorn with fourteen ships, including one Neapolitan ship and the *Agamemnon.* When the French sighted the British lookout frigates, they quickly changed course and headed back toward Toulon. The frigates reported their movements to Hotham's main force. By the morning of March 12, the British ships-of-the-line came within sight of the French. At the mercy of the baffling winds, they could not manage to close for action.

On the morning of March 13, the wind freshened and Hotham hoisted a signal for a "general chase." This gave Nelson the opportunity to use the *Agamemnon*'s best speed, sailing independently of the others. Since she was one of the fastest sailers in the fleet, the *Agamemnon* managed to be well in the van. The lead Nelson held over the other British ships soon increased, and he quickly took the first chance to engage the larger French ships.

Nelson's great fighting spirit had been well demonstrated during the fighting ashore at San Juan, Bastia, and Calvi. This was the first time that he would have an opportunity to show what he could do in a major fleet action.

Squally winds had snapped the topmasts of one of the French ships. The third from the rear, a big 80-gun French ship, the *Ca Ira,* slammed into the stern of another ship with landlubberly clumsiness. This collision with the ship ahead toppled the fore and main topmasts of the *Ca Ira.* They crashed down and dangled over the lee side. The stricken French ship lost a good spread of canvas to the wind, and the tangled wreckage dragging through the water slowed her down. The fouled masts, lines, and sail prevented the *Ca Ira* from firing her portside batteries.

Meanwhile, the British frigate *Inconstant,* under Captain Fremantle, had gone straight for the *Ca Ira,* and opened fire on her before the *Agamemnon* arrived. The return fire from the big French ship, however, was too overwhelming for a frigate, and the *Inconstant* was forced to withdraw.

Soon after ten o'clock, the *Ca Ira* dropped astern of her formation. The *Agamemnon* closed for action, and readied her guns for battle. As the ships drew closer, Nelson could see how much bigger the French ship was—"absolutely large enough to take *Agamemnon* in her hold."

By now, the crippled *Ca Ira* was under tow by a French frigate, and could not maneuver to bring her broadside guns to bear. However, she greeted the *Agamemnon* with accurate fire from her six stern guns.

"Not a shot missed some part of the ship," Nelson recorded, "and laterally the masts were struck every shot, which obliged me to open fire a few minutes sooner than I intended."

Nelson brought *Agamemnon* up close to the enemy

stern. He skillfully gave orders to his men at the helm and aloft to turn the ship broadside to the *Ca Ira.* "As the ship fell off (the wind), we gave her our whole broadside, each gun doubled-shotted," wrote Nelson.

The *Agamemnon* alternately raked the *Ca Ira* with her guns, and then chased her to make up the lost distance. The cannon progressively damaged the ship. Nelson's ship was so far ahead of the others, that she was the only one engaged.

Alone, the huge 80-gun *Ca Ira* was more than the 64-gun *Agamemnon* could normally handle—but she was not alone. Nearby were two huge French ships—one of them, the *Sans Culotte,* with one hundred and twenty guns.

Strangely enough, however, the other big French ships did not once drop back to help the *Ca Ira.* Then, at one o'clock, the entire French Fleet turned back to assist. By this time, fortunately, the British Fleet was also closing the scene. Hotham sent a signal of recall to Nelson—the smaller *Agamemnon* was no match for the *Ca Ira,* let alone the whole French Fleet!

At dawn the next morning, the *Censeur,* a line-of-battle ship which had taken the crippled *Ca Ira* in tow, was still struggling along far behind the rest of the French Fleet. The huge *Sans Culotte* had made a bee-line for home, and was completely out of sight! This earned her captain a court-martial.

During the morning the fickle winds played games with the two fleets. At last a breeze came up, and the British were able to cut off the *Censeur* and the *Ca Ira* from the rest of the French Fleet.

Hotham then decided to send only two of his 74-gun ships, the *Captain* and the *Bedford*, to attack them. They soon learned that the *Ca Ira*, though crippled in her rigging, was perfectly sound in her powerful batteries! Before long, the two British men-of-war were battered out of action. Too late, Hotham discovered that he should have sent in a stronger force.

Soon the two main fleets were again within firing range of each other, and a few shots were exchanged. At this point, the French admiral decided to withdraw from action. The battered *Ca Ira* and the *Censeur* were left behind to shift for themselves. About ten in the morning, Nelson brought the *Agamemnon* alongside, and claimed them for Great Britain.

As the French Fleet hauled off toward the horizon, Admiral Hotham's flagship, the 100-gun *Britannia*, came up behind the *Agamemnon*. Vice Admiral Goodall, the next ranking officer, drew ahead in his flagship, the 90-gun *Princess Royal*. Noticing that Hotham had no intention of pursuing the French, Nelson ordered his boat lowered and rowed over to Admiral Hotham's flagship. He hoped to persuade Hotham to change his mind.

Nelson was like a "tiger on a leash"—and the leash was held by his Commander-in-chief. The old and ailing Admiral tried to calm Nelson down: "We must be contented, we have done very well."

Admiral Goodall supported Nelson, but Hotham seemed satisfied with his small victory. He felt that, whatever plans the enemy fleet may have had, "their intentions are for the present frustrated."

"Had we taken ten sail," Nelson remarked, "and

allowed the eleventh to escape, when it had been possible to have got her, I could never have called it well done. We should have had such a day as the annals of England never produced."

At any rate, the French Fleet disappeared over the horizon—and it was to plague the British for years. Hotham had managed to blunder again—losing another golden opportunity to defeat the French. Needless to say, Nelson was given no credit in Hotham's official report to the Admiralty.

"What has happened may never happen to anyone again," Nelson wrote, "that only one ship-of-the-line out of fourteen should get into action with the French Fleet for so long a time as two-hours-and-a-half, and with such a ship as the *Ca Ira.*"

After his encounter with the *Ca Ira,* Nelson sailed in the *Agamemnon* on July 4, with six smaller ships on detached duty. He was to assist General de Vins, the Commander-in-chief of the Austrian Army, by stopping French shipping along the Italian Riviera.

Two days later, while en route, Nelson sailed straight into the jaws of the French Fleet, which now consisted of seventeen sail-of-the-line. By outsailing the entire fleet he managed to escape capture, and slipped into the fleet anchorage at San Fiorenzo. By the time Hotham's ships, then under maintenance and repair, could go to sea, the French Fleet had disappeared.

On the morning of July 13, the French Fleet again was sighted. Hotham managed to fritter away several hours by changing positions in his own line of ships, while the French drew away out of range. When Hotham finally ordered a general chase, the eager *Agamemnon* and the *Captain* were in the lead.

Since the British ships were astern of the French line, the firing was restricted to the bow and stern guns. However, a shift of the wind suddenly threw them broadside to, and heavy firing began. The *Alcide*, the last ship in the French line, took the worst beating as round-shot crashed into her hull and rigging. About two o'clock in the afternoon she was forced to strike her colors, but she blew up before she could be captured.

During the chase and battle, the *Britannia*, one of the slowest sailers in the fleet, fell behind eight miles. Admiral Hotham could not see the action at that distance and, in typical fashion, he ordered a recall. Time and again his "leadership" prevented decisive actions, and passed on the problems of the French Fleet to subsequent commanders.

After this action with the French Fleet, Nelson and the *Agamemnon* were sent off again to assist General de Vins. Admiral Hotham was only too glad to get the spirited, supercharged Nelson off by himself where he could no longer show up his own feeble ambitions in combat.

For his distinguished service at Bastia and Calvi, Nelson had recently been made an "honorary Colonel" of Marines. He felt that the rank was more than just honorary.

"Here I am," he wrote, "having commenced cooperation with an old Austrian general, almost fancying myself charging at the head of a troop of horses!"

Nelson did his best to stop the coastal shipping, so vital to the invading armies of Napoleon. He found the task a difficult one with his rickety ships and his exhausted men. Keen judgment was also required because of the neutral nations involved.

Describing one action to Hotham, Nelson reported: "A convoy of provisions and ammunition arrived at Alassio, a place in the possession of the French army. Yesterday I proceeded with the ships named in the margin to that place, where, within an hour, we took the vessels named in the enclosed list.

"There was a very feeble opposition from some of the enemy's cavalry, who fired on our boats after boarding the vessels near shore, but I have the pleasure to say no man was killed or wounded. The enemy had two thousand horse and foot soldiers in the town, which prevented my landing and destroying their magazines of provisions and ammunition.

"I sent Captain Fremantle in the *Inconstant*, with the *Tartar*, to Languelia, a town on the west side of the Bay of Alassio, where he executed my orders in the most officer-like manner. I am indebted to every Captain and Officer of the Squadron for their activity."

On November 24, the Austrian and French troops clashed in a battle at Vado Bay, near Genoa. Shortly after the battle started, General de Vins left his command because of illness.

From then on, the Austrian retreat turned into a rout, and the entire coast fell into the hands of the French. Two thousand French troops planned to sail down the coast, and cut off the escaping Austrians. With his usual brilliance, Nelson prevented this by anchoring the *Agamemnon* across the harbor entrance at Genoa.

With no Austrian army left to support, the *Agamemnon* sailed for Leghorn. Here the exhausted crew rested and the ship was refitted.

Disrupting the flow of supplies to Napoleon's

armies would now be a bigger task than ever. Hotham had never given Nelson an adequate force to support the Austrian army. His repeated requests for more ships were answered with a reduction in his squadron, and the additional duty of reconnoitering the harbor of Toulon. All the while as the weeks drifted by, the British ships were peacefully swinging around their anchors at Leghorn.

The saving grace of an admiral's authority to blunder on and on is the traditional rotation of duty. Then the blunderers go on to other stations, free to muddle through again, leaving their troubles behind to those who have to carry on. In this way, before conditions become utterly hopeless, the good sooner or later relieve the bad. So it was with Admiral Hotham.

When Hotham hauled down his flag in the *Britannia* on the first of November, there was little improvement under the temporary command of Sir Hyde Parker.

"Admiral Hotham kept my squadron too small for its duty," Nelson later wrote, "and the moment Sir Hyde Parker took command of the fleet, he reduced it to nothing—only one frigate and a brig—whereas I requested two 74-gun ships, and eight or ten frigates, to insure safety to the army."

To add to Nelson's woes, a report had been sent to the Secretary of State for Foreign Affairs, stating that captains of British ships of war had been guilty of conniving with port officials over the entry of supply ships into French-held ports. Nelson's indignation now moved him to fight with words as well as with ships.

"I do demand," he replied to the Secretary, "that

the person, whoever he may be, that wrote or gave that paper to your Lordship, do fully, and expressly bring home his charge. He states that this agreement is made by numbers of people on both sides. We dare him, my Lord, to the proof. If he cannot, I do most humbly implore, that His Majesty will be most graciously pleased to direct his Attorney General to prosecute this infamous libeller in His Courts of Law.

"If true, no punishment can be too great for the traitors; if false, none can be too heavy for the villain, who has dared to allow his pen to write such a paper."

By the end of 1795, after many months of "rough sailing," better days were ahead for Nelson. One of England's greatest admirals—Sir John Jervis—was soon to become the Commander-in-chief in the Mediterranean.

CHAPTER EIGHT

"AS FIT FOR SEA AS A ROTTEN SHIP CAN BE"

The *Agamemnon* bustled with activity during December of 1795. After arriving at Leghorn on the sixth of the month, the crew turned to, repairing her masts, sails, and hull in order to make her "as fit for sea as a rotten ship can be."

Underway again in January, the *Agamemnon* sailed into San Fiorenzo Bay, where Sir John Jervis' flagship was anchored. An important meeting was about to take place between Nelson and his new Commander-in-chief.

Admiral Jervis was a "man of business." He was also known to be a strict disciplinarian and a man of action. Sir John sent a shiver down many a spine with his piercing blue eyes. They looked directly at a person, seeking out the truth like an X ray. News of his arrival in the Mediterranean caused mixed feelings in the fleet—gone were the days of peacefully riding at anchor in port.

The new Commander-in-chief had heard of Nelson's exploits in the Mediterranean. As the shrill whistle of the bo'sun's pipe announced his arrival, Nelson climbed up the side of the flagship. Jervis eagerly sized up the Captain of the *Agamemnon,* about whom he had heard so much.

Actually, Admiral Jervis, who always kept a sharp ear and eye on personal performance, had already formed an opinion of Nelson's character. Nelson had been cheated out of proper mention in almost every official report. Nevertheless, he was often the topic of lively conversation in every wardroom of the fleet, and at every taproom where seamen gathered. Even at the Admiralty, the dull official reports of combat contrasted strangely with the glowing tales of eyewitness accounts. Nelson's name was becoming well-known by the best means of communication in the sailing navy—the fleet grapevine.

"I joined Sir John Jervis yesterday," wrote Nelson, "and was received not only with the greatest attention, but with much apparent friendship. I found the Admiral anxious to know many things which, I was not a little surprised, had not been communicated to him from others of the Fleet.

"It would appear he was well satisfied with my opinion of what is likely to happen. He had no reserves with me of his information, opinions, and thoughts. He concluded by asking if I had any objection to serve under him with my flag."

Nelson was soon promoted to Commodore. As a flag officer, his own distinguishing pennant would fly from whatever ship he sailed in. The promotion proved that Jervis realized Nelson was especially capable, and that he planned to call on him for future assignments of importance. This Admiral Jervis later did, often ignoring the jealously-guarded seniority of other officers in his command.

"You did just as you pleased in Lord Hood's time," one of the captains complained to Nelson, "the same in Admiral Hotham's, and now again with Sir John Jervis—it makes no difference to you who is Commander-in-chief."

Admiral Jervis immediately supplied Nelson with additional ships to carry on his patrol duties along the French and Italian coasts.

"Our squadron at present consists of two sail-of-the-line and four frigates, but is to be increased in the summer," a young midshipman named Hoste wrote home from the *Agamemnon*. "We shall not want for amusement, I have no doubt, as our Commodore Nelson does not like to be idle."

On April 4 Nelson hoisted his commodore's pennant in the *Agamemnon*. The *Agamemnon*'s crew returned to the familiar task of intercepting and interrupting the supply line to Napoleon's troops. They were kept busy chasing the supply ships along the Riviera, and exchanging shots with the increasing number of shore batteries.

On May 31, Nelson's squadron captured two small warships and five transports, carrying siege guns and equipment, bound for Mantua. This was a blow to Napoleon's forces but, by now, his army was rolling along relentlessly over all opposition.

A new era began on June 11 when Nelson shifted his broad commodore's pennant to the 74-gun HMS *Captain*. The *Agamemnon*, which had gained immortality with Nelson in many a sea chase and campaign, had "sailed admirably," but she was now worn-out after more than three years under Nelson's command. As she departed from San Fiorenzo Bay with a convoy bound for England, she was no longer the fast, smart ship Nelson had once known. Her hull was bound together by cables. As she and the frigate *Meleager* sailed away together, Nelson had to admit that they looked "like two tubs floating on the water."

With his pennant flying from the mast of the *Captain*, Nelson would no longer be the captain of a single ship. He would be in command of a group of ships when assigned to a squadron.

Commodore Nelson had signed on many of his *Agamemnon* ship's company in the *Captain*. Her commanding officer was Captain Ralph Miller, and her First Lieutenant was Edward Berry. On board all was well, with good prospects for lively action under their new fleet commander.

Nelson continued his operations along the Riviera in the *Captain*, doing what he could to intercept the French at sea. On land, Napoleon's soldiers rolled across the plains of Italy. Leghorn fell so quickly that many British subjects had no chance to leave.

One English family, the Wynnes, with their four daughters, had just fled from Florence to Leghorn a week earlier. On June 20, they quickly finished breakfast, rushed down to the dock, and embarked in the frigate *Inconstant*, under Captain Fremantle.

Charming eighteen-year-old Betsy Wynne kept a diary, and described "a most terrible bustle and noise—all packing up and getting on board the ships." The inconvenience of being whisked aboard ship was soon forgotten, as Betsy fell in love with the ship's captain.

"I found the *Inconstant* so fine, so clean and comfortable," she confided in her diary. "I was quite delighted, and regretted no more the French had obliged us to run away.

"How kind and amiable Captain Fremantle is—he pleases me more than any man I have yet seen. The Captain, though excessively busy and persecuted by everybody, took the greatest pains to amuse us."

Betsy repeatedly betrayed her heart to her diary.

"As long as we stay on board the *Inconstant* with this excellent man, I do not care what part of the world we go to."

Betsy was very unhappy when the Wynnes were transferred to the first-rate ship-of-the-line *Britannia.* The spacious flag officer's quarters were theirs, but it did little to console her over the separation from Captain Fremantle.

"Every time I hear a strange boat is in sight I feel my heart beat with double force," Betsy wrote.

One day the officers of the *Britannia* reported a ship in sight which looked like the *Inconstant.* However, it turned out to be the frigate *Sardine.*

"A most cruel pain seized my heart," she wrote. "I blushed and turned pale—it was at the table and did not pass unnoticed."

The pain of separation finally ended one happy day in October, when the *Inconstant* rejoined the fleet. Although Captain Foley of the *Britannia* had hopes of winning her, true love could not be denied, and the Wynnes consented to the marriage of Captain Fremantle and their daughter. Betsy's diary added many sidelights to the Navy of Nelson's day.

The overall situation in the Mediterranean was growing gloomier each month. Napoleon's forces swept down the Italian peninsula, closing the ports of Naples and Sicily to the British ships. Nelson began the blockade of the port of Leghorn on the seventh of July.

By September, the Spanish threatened to join France, and Admiral Jervis received orders to withdraw from the Mediterranean. Nelson's squadron was sent to evacuate the British forces from Bastia—the fortress taken with such great courage and effort two years before.

The inhabitants of Corsica were unfriendly—they could see the danger of siding with a loser. Nelson brought three ships-of-the-line up to the breakwater of the town. He then notified the officials that if anything were done to interfere with the evacuation of troops and supplies, he would blast the town to bits.

"Nothing shall be left undone that ought to be done," he promised Admiral Jervis, "even if it should be necessary to knock down Bastia."

A large force of French troops landed at nearby Cape Corso on October 18, and threatened to halt the evacuation. On the following day they sent a written demand that the British troops should not be permitted to embark in the ships. While the demands and replies were going back and forth, the British wasted no time. Under Nelson's supervision, they loaded one hundred tons of cannon, supplies and provisions by sunset! At six o'clock on the following morning, as the last of the troops and supplies embarked, Nelson and the commanding general shoved off from Bastia in a barge.

"I am happy to say that not only Bastia, but every other place in the Island is completely evacuated," Nelson wrote to the Duke of Clarence. "The enemy was in one end of Bastia, before we had quitted the other. The exertions of the Navy on this occasion, as on all others I have seen, have been great.

"We have now done with Corsica. Its inhabitants are so greedy of wealth and so jealous of each other, that it would require the patience of Job and the riches of Croesus to satisfy them."

Twenty Spanish ships-of-the-line were off Cape Corso, when the British ships set sail before a brisk wind for Elba. There they unloaded supplies at Porto Ferrajo for the British garrison. The *Captain* then sailed for Gibraltar to join the main fleet.

At Gibraltar, Nelson was greeted with orders to evacuate Elba. A few days later, on December 15, he sailed back into the Mediterranean—now enemy territory. To avoid being overtaken by the Spanish or French Fleets, Jervis put two fast frigates under his command—the *Minerve* and the *Blanche*. With his pennant fluttering from the mast of the *Minerve*, Nelson sailed "on a most important mission, which with God's blessing, I have little doubt of accomplishing."

His important mission was to evacuate Elba—but it almost foundered en route. Nelson could not resist engaging two Spanish frigates sighted near Cartagena an hour before midnight on December 19. They paired off against each other in a lively exchange of fire.

By 1:30 A.M., after a brave fight, *La Sabina* surrendered to Nelson. The Spanish ship was taken as a prize and a British crew was placed on board. Don Jacobo Stuart, her captain, surrendered his sword as he was taken prisoner aboard the *Minerve*. The badly crippled *La Sabina* was then taken in tow.

In the meantime, the *Blanche* had defeated the other ship. At 3:30 A.M., a third Spanish frigate arrived on the scene, and was engaged by the *Blanche*. The crew could not board the defeated ship, because she was still fighting the second frigate.

Dawn suddenly revealed two Spanish ships-of-the-line bearing down on them! The *Minerve* and the *Blanche* were in a predicament! Their masts and rigging were torn and shattered so badly they could hardly get enough sail to the wind to avoid being captured by the big Spanish men-of-war. *La Sabina* had been cast loose and was recaptured by the Spanish, with the British officers, Lieutenants Hardy and Culverhouse, still on board.

Finally eluding his Spanish pursuers, Nelson continued on to Elba where his ships were repaired. There he embarked Sir Gilbert Elliot, former Viceroy of Corsica, and his staff, including Colonel John Drinkwater. However, Army General De Burgh, in command of the troops on Elba, said he had received no instructions to leave, and refused to evacuate his troops!

On his way back to Gibraltar, Nelson reconnoitered the French and Spanish ports to inform Admiral Jervis. Near the Bay of Gibraltar, he noticed a number of Spanish ships and decided to grasp the opportunity to arrange for an exchange of prisoners.

"The fortune of war put *La Sabina* into my possession, after she had been most gallantly defended

—the fickle dame returned her to you with some of my officers and men in her," Nelson wrote to the Captain General at Cartagena.

"I consent, Sir, that Don Jacobo may be exchanged, and with full liberty to serve his King, when Lieutenants Culverhouse and Hardy are delivered into the garrison of Gibraltar, with such others as may be agreed on. It becomes great nations to act with generosity to each other, and to soften the horrors of war."

This letter brought about the exchange of prisoners. Nelson had treated Don Jacobo Stuart with great courtesy, and had returned his sword, while he was aboard the *Minerve*. However, he added one more touch—a letter to the Spanish Admiral Don Juan Marino.

"I cannot allow Don Jacobo to return to you without expressing my admiration of his gallant conduct. To you, who have seen the state of his ship, it is needless to mention the impossibility of her longer defence. I have lost many brave men, but in our masts [not breaking] I was most fortunate—or, probably, I should have had the honor of your acquaintance!"

Commodore Nelson sailed out of Gibraltar on February 11, 1797, to join Admiral Jervis' main fleet off the coast of Portugal. As he fought to clear the shelter of the Rock of Gibraltar, which blocked the wind from his sails, two Spanish ships-of-the-line sailed in pursuit. The ships were so close to land that spectators from the town and the garrison crowded along the hills to watch the battle.

The *Minerve* was still in the lee of the huge Rock while the Spanish, farther out at sea, were enjoying a steadier breeze, and gaining. As she drew near, the leading Spanish warship cleared her decks for action.

Colonel Drinkwater was on deck watching the Spanish ships astern. Nodding toward his colors, Nelson said to him: "Before the Dons get hold of that bunting I will have a struggle with them, and sooner than give up the frigate, I'll run her ashore."

The *Minerve* picked up a little breeze, and gained some distance. Dinner was announced, and the officers went below to the wardroom. The Colonel, meeting Hardy, congratulated him on his return to the ship. Just then there came a shout from the deck.

"Man overboard!"

Lieutenant Thomas Hardy bolted out of the wardroom, and was soon being lowered into one of the ship's boats. The situation was perilous—the Spanish ships could again close the distance, unless the *Minerve* set full sail immediately for the Atlantic.

"By God, I'll not lose Hardy!" Nelson exclaimed. "Back the mizzen-topsail."

This maneuver to check the ship's speed was also apparent to the Spanish man-of-war. It confounded the Spanish captain! He cautiously checked his own speed—thinking the British Fleet might be coming from over the horizon. The Spanish ships promptly changed course and headed back toward Gibraltar!

Although the sailor who had fallen overboard could not be found, Hardy's boat returned, and was hoisted aboard. The *Minerve* continued peacefully on her way—it was a close call!

The Pillars of Hercules, two promontories of land forming the gateway into the Mediterranean, dropped farther astern of the *Minerve*. As Commodore Nelson sailed out of the Mediterranean, there was not a single British man-of-war inside the "gateway." Behind him he left a hostile sea. Ahead stretched the broad Atlantic. Through the ocean swells the *Minerve* plowed and pitched toward new adventures.

CHAPTER NINE

"WESTMINSTER ABBEY OR VICTORY"

Clouds of dust rising from Napoleon's marching legions marked his relentless advance over cities and sovereignties. People were paralyzed with fear over the legend of his invincibility. By force and threat, Napoleon succeeded in closing port after port in the Mediterranean to British ships. As Nelson sailed into a foggy night to rendezvous with Admiral Jervis' fleet, the outlook for the British looked grim both on land and sea.

Far from friendly shores, the British Mediterranean Fleet was in dire straits for food, water, and supplies. The ships had to sail long distances for repairs, and many of them were badly in need of rope, tar, thread, timber, and other naval supplies. Some of the ships could hardly make the voyage back to England with fair winds, and with no enemies to battle along the way.

Reporting the desperate situation, Admiral Jervis wrote to the Admiralty: "The *Tarleton* is in such wretched condition that I tremble for Lord Proby, his officers and crew. The mainmast of the *Egmont* was reported to be in danger of going over at the first gale of wind.

"The *Poulette*: Her decks, waterways, bottom between wind and water, and lower masts, are much decayed, together with an entire want of sails and cordage. The sloop cannot with safety undertake a passage back to England.

"The *Belotte*: Altogether in such a crazy and infirm state, as to be totally incapable of a passage back to England."

For the hard-pressed British Fleet, disaster and discouragement piled upon each other in an overwhelming avalanche. A lesser man than Admiral Jervis would surely have broken under the strain. When HMS *Courageux* was wrecked with the loss of all hands, Jervis reported: "At any time the loss of such a ship would have been very great, but in the present circumstances of my force, compared with that of the enemy, it is beyond all calculation."

Slowly the strangulation of supplies to the British ships was complete. A desperately needed supply of hemp from Leghorn was permanently cut off. To keep his creaking ships together, Jervis pleaded with Sir William Hamilton, the British Ambassador at Naples, for "a great supply of nails, elm and oak board, lead and leather. But above all, we are in the greatest distress for sewing twine, our only resource now being in drawing threads from our canvas." Sir William, however, could not manage to get supplies out of the port of Naples because of tight French control.

The buildup of the enemy was not confined to Napoleon's land armies alone. The French and Spanish squadrons were overwhelmingly larger and in better condition than those of the Royal Navy. The French Fleet alone numbered thirty or more ships-of-the-line.

All of this would seem bad enough, but Admiral Jervis was to suffer another incomprehensible blow—desertion! Desertion in the Navy was not unknown for one man, or even a group of men. However, Jervis was struck speechless when he heard the disastrous news that Admiral Man—and his whole fleet of seven ships—had set sail for home!

Admiral Jervis was magnificently restrained in his dispatch to the Admiralty upon hearing this incredible news. He felt that he should have realized how close Admiral Man had been to a nervous breakdown, sailing for months in the shadow of the huge French and Spanish Fleets. Needless to say, upon reaching England, Admiral Man was ordered to haul down his flag for the last time.

The situation of the British Mediterranean Fleet would have been impossible had Jervis and his captains not succeeded in capturing prize ships from the enemy. During the first few months of Admiral Jervis' command, over fifty merchant ships were captured, providing such supplies as grain, wines, cloth, needles, awls, leather, brandy, bread, and guns.

Another asset to the Fleet was the superiority of British seamanship and discipline. It also helped to have Portugal join the side of the British. This increased Jervis' force by seven ships, sailing under Portuguese command. They might not have cast their lot with the British had they known in what poor condition their allies' ships were.

In January, 1797, Admiral William Parker arrived from England with five ships-of-the-line. However, misfortune had struck on the voyage southward. The *Colossus* lost her mainmast and, when it came crashing down, it wrecked other topside rigging. She was in no condition for battle without in-port repairs.

Admiral Parker's opinion of the condition of the British ships was so dismal that he felt they were "too weak to do much with the Spanish Fleet if they should put to sea." Little did he know they would engage the Spanish Fleet in battle in only two weeks! He also did not realize the overriding force of Nelson's fighting spirit.

The extensive preparations of the French and Spanish Fleets, and the massing of men and arms, were bound to burst forth into a battle. Realizing this, Jervis sent a dispatch to Parker informing him that Nelson was escorting troopships and storeships past Gibraltar.

"I must be in a position to go speedily to his assistance in case the Spanish Fleet attempts to interrupt his passage. I shall therefore cruise off Cape St. Vincent. Join me as soon as possible."

The Spaniards had departed from their naval base at Cartagena about February 1, and were sailing toward the Straits of Gibraltar to rendezvous with the French Fleet at Brest. The combined forces then planned to convey Napoleon's army across the Channel to invade England.

Thus the stage was set for the Battle off Cape St. Vincent. The British people did not realize on what a thin thread their country's security dangled!

Before Nelson joined the Fleet, he was due for

more adventure. The same night on which he escaped from the Spanish near Gibraltar, the *Minerve* fell in with a large company of strange ships during the night. He sailed into their formation in the fog, his identity unknown! By maneuvering with them, he escaped from the Spanish Fleet undetected! This gave him information about the location of the Spanish Fleet, and he learned that they were heading up the coast toward Cádiz.

The *Minerve* safely rejoined the fleet on February 13, and Nelson shifted his flag back to the *Captain*.

Admiral Jervis' fleet guarded the Atlantic approaches to Gibraltar as he cruised off Cape St. Vincent. The Cape, a sharp prong of land jutting southwestward into the Atlantic, forms a corner of Portugal. When the Spanish Fleet rounded the corner, the British hoped to surprise them!

As darkness fell on February 13, no sign of a Spanish sail had appeared. Then, during the night, a shift of the wind brought distinct sounds announcing the arrival of the Spanish Fleet. To keep in formation and avoid collision while sailing through the fog, they were firing their minute guns.

Admiral Jervis paced the deck of the *Victory* nearly all night long. At 5:30 the next morning, Captain Edward Foote of the lookout frigate *Niger* reported the Spanish Fleet very near.

"A victory to England is very essential at this moment!" Jervis exclaimed to those around him on the quarterdeck.

Through the chilly, damp dawn, the huge shapes of the Spanish ships filtered through the curtain of hazy fog. Captain Ben Hallowell stood next to Admiral

Jervis on the quarterdeck, his eyes straining through the mist for sight of the enemy.

"There are eight sail-of-the-line, Sir John."

"Very well, sir," Jervis replied.

"There are twenty sail-of-the-line, Sir John."

"Very well, sir."

"There are twenty-five sail-of-the-line, Sir John."

"Very well, sir."

"There are *twenty-seven* sail-of-the-line, Sir John!"

"Enough, sir. No more of that! If there are *fifty* sail, I will go through them."

Momentarily forgetting Sir John's rank, Captain Hallowell thumped him on the back in his enthusiasm.

"That's right, Sir John, that's right! And by God, we'll give them a damned good licking!"

With obvious satisfaction, the Admiral observed his fifteen ships sailing along in a tight formation in two orderly columns. They contrasted sharply with the straggling order of the Spanish Grand Fleet, under Admiral Cordoba, as it emerged from the haze. Nine of the Spanish ships were separated by miles from the other eighteen.

At 10:45, Jervis quickly hoisted a signal—his fleet would sail in a line through the gap, and separate the nine stragglers from the main force. In the lead was Captain Troubridge in the *Culloden.* The *Victory,* with Admiral Jervis and Captain Robert Calder, was in the middle of the line. Commodore Nelson and Captain Ralph Miller were third from the end in the *Captain.*

First to open fire was the *Culloden,* who blasted a broadside at the first Spaniard to pass. As she sailed ahead, the *Culloden* was bearing down on a huge three-decker Spanish ship—on a collision course! Troubridge boldly held course, and when the Spaniard went about, he blasted her with two double-loaded precisely timed broadsides.

The *Culloden* sailed on past the Spanish formation, to the end of the Spanish line. Anticipating a turn signal from the Admiral, Troubridge had his repeater flags ready to hoist, and stood by to turn his helm. When the turn signal went up on the *Victory,* Troubridge answered so quickly that Jervis could not help but notice it.

"Look at Troubridge!" he exclaimed. "He tacks his ship to battle as if the eyes of all England were upon him—and would to God they were!"

As the other British ships came within range, a heavy exchange of fire roared out from both Spanish and British ships. On the deck of the *Victory,* Admiral Jervis was splattered with the blood of a nearby marine who was killed on the quarterdeck. Staff Captain Grey, thinking the Admiral wounded, ran up to see what he could do.

"I am not at all hurt," Sir John assured him, and calmly added, "But do you, George, see if you can get me an orange."

As the British ships turned, following each other in line, their formation assumed a "J" shape. The eighteen Spanish ships, seeing a clear stretch of water, set sail with every inch of canvas to escape—attempting to join their leeward group of nine ships. If they had succeeded, this would have ended the fighting with nothing more than a skirmish.

The Spanish threatened to slip away from the British. Four of the big Spanish ships, racing for the open stretch of water, were sailing tightly grouped from the others. One was the huge flagship *Santissima Trinidad,* a four-decker ship-of-the-line, considered to be the largest and heaviest-gunned ship in the world!

Nelson's *Captain* was near the top of the "J." Instinctively, and without orders, he turned his ship out of the line, and sailed the *Captain* across the course of the huge ships! It was then about one o'clock in the afternoon.

The *Culloden,* still leading the line, was at the other end of the "J." Captain Troubridge, a sailor after Nelson's heart, quickly brought his ship out of the line to support the *Captain.*

From the deck of the *Victory,* Jervis observed this unauthorized departure from battle procedure with more than lively interest! Astonished at such a bold move, Captain Calder pleaded with the Admiral to recall Nelson.

"No," replied Sir John, "I will not have them recalled. I put my faith in those ships."

Nelson's bold action threw the Spanish into confusion, and forced them to give up all thought of joining their other group of ships. They turned to the north, and lost valuable distance. The *Prince George* (Admiral Parker's flagship), the *Orion, Blenheim,* and *Excellent* were then able to catch up with the escaping Spaniards.

Until the *Culloden* arrived, the superior Spanish fire-power hammered the *Captain* unmercifully. The *Santissima Trinidad* carried 130 guns, the *San Josef* and *Salvador Del Mundo* mounted 112 guns each, and the *San Nicolas* was an 84-gun ship. The devastating barrage from their broadside cannon was deafening. While Nelson's ship returned the fire magnificently, she was no match for the huge Spanish ships.

When the *Culloden* and *Blenheim* arrived, they opened up with heavy fire, giving the *Captain* welcome support. Captain Collingwood, in the *Excellent,* drew near the *San Nicolas* and fired a broadside into the ship. This slowed down the Spaniards' firing, caused the ship to veer off course, and she crunched into the side of the huge *San Josef.*

The *Captain* was so battered that she was in poor sailing condition and hard to handle. Collingwood had arrived at an opportune moment to help Nelson.

"He most gallantly pushed up, with every sail set, to save his old friend and messmate."

The *Excellent* then sailed on in hot pursuit of the *Santissima Trinidad.*

Any other officer might have considered this glory enough for one day, and withdrawn while his ship still was holding together. However, Nelson was just getting warmed up! By crowding on every rag of canvas the *Captain* could hold to the wind, Nelson ordered Captain Miller to deliberately ram the *San Nicolas*!

"Her spritsail yard passing over the enemy's poop deck, and hooking her mizzen shrouds," observed Colonel Drinkwater from the frigate *Lively.*

"At this time," recalled Nelson, "the *Captain* having lost her fore-topmast, not a sail, shroud, or rope standing, her wheel shot away, and incapable of further service in the Line, or in chase, I directed Captain Miller to put the helm a-starboard. Calling for boarders, I ordered them to board."

The two ships were rammed together, and held entangled in the rigging. Commander Berry leaped into action, and was the first to board the *San Nicolas*. Following closely behind him were Lieutenant Pierson and soldiers of the Sixty-ninth Regiment who were serving as marines. Captain Miller started to lead another group aboard, but Nelson stopped him.

"No, Miller," he called out over the din, "I must have that honor myself!"

Nelson climbed over the stern of the *San Nicolas*. He ordered a marine of the Sixty-ninth Regiment to smash one of the quarter gallery windows with the butt of his rifle, and they jumped into an officer's cabin. The cabin doors to the decks were locked, but quickly smashed open, while the Spanish officers fired their pistols at them through the windows.

After a volley of musket fire, the Spanish fell back, and Nelson and his band of boarders bounded up to the quarter deck. By this time, Berry had taken possession of the poop deck, and was busy hauling down the Spanish colors.

Hurrying forward along the deck, Nelson encountered three Spanish officers, captured by his marines. As they surrendered their swords to him, a lively crackling of musket and pistol fire from the port side drew their attention. Snipers from the *San Josef,* a huge three-decker, were firing at them from the rail of the stern galleries which towered above them.

Calling for reinforcements from the *Captain,* Nelson stationed men at the hatchways to keep the Spaniards belowdecks, and led another group of boarders to the *San Josef*! Berry charged along with Nelson. As they climbed over the rail of the lower deck, Nelson shouted:

"Westminster Abbey or victory!"

Nelson felt confident of victory, rather than a hero's burial at Westminster Abbey!

While they raced toward the quarterdeck, a Spanish officer leaned over the rail, and called out that the ship surrendered. The captain of the *San Josef* bowed to Nelson, and handed over his sword. Then, he informed Nelson that his Admiral, Don Xavier Francisco Winthuysen, was dying of his wounds belowdecks.

"On the quarter-deck of a Spanish first-rate," recorded Nelson, "extravagant as the story may seem, did I receive the swords of the vanquished Spaniards —which, as I received, I gave to William Fearney, one of my bargemen, who put them with the greatest sangfroid under his arm."

With the three ships lashed together, Nelson's "brave fellows" were thinly spread over the *Captain, San Nicholas,* and the *San Josef.* Valor and bravery has its price—the *Captain* suffered the heaviest casualties of the British Fleet. However, her losses were small when compared with the 500 killed and wounded in the *Santissima Trinidad.*

The Spanish Fleet, after losing four ships-of-the-line, the *San Nicolas, San Josef, San Ysidro,* and the *Salvador Del Mundo,* fled to the port of Cádiz.

Nelson returned to his ship to present Captain Miller with the captain's sword of the *San Nicolas.* When he found his own cabin an absolute wreck, he later shifted his flag temporarily to the *Irresistible.*

It was the spark of Nelson's genius, and his boldness, which ignited the Battle off Cape St. Vincent. Without him, there would have been no battle. Once the battle began, however, his fellow officers pitched in with a spirit which complemented that of Nelson himself.

Late in the afternoon after the battle, each ship passed by, the British sailors waving and cheering madly.

"The *Victory* passed the *Captain,* saluting with three cheers, as did every ship in the Fleet," showing their admiration for Nelson's inspiring action.

Nelson then was rowed over to the *Victory* to report to Admiral Jervis, and to review the events of the day. As he climbed up the ship's side and stepped onto the deck, he was still blackened from the gunsmoke. The tattered remains of his uniform were as ragged as the flapping shreds of sail clinging to the spars on his ship.

Nelson's cocked hat, shot through with holes, would have triggered a gale of laughter on any other occasion! It made no difference now, as he walked across the deck to meet Sir John. Everyone was already laughing and cheering on the crest of victory. Even "Old Oak," as Admiral Jervis was called, was unusually demonstrative. He slapped Nelson on the back, and greeted him with elation and words of admiration.

Without orders, Nelson had veered out of the line of battle, right under the eyes of his Commander-in-chief, whose motto was "Obedience, Obedience, Obedience." This kind of disobedience, however, Jervis approved of! Nelson's brilliant fighting off Cape St. Vincent was at first daring—then amazing, and finally inspiring.

That evening, as the officers talked over the events

of the day, Captain Calder of the *Victory* was still of the opinion that Nelson should be reprimanded for acting without orders! He grumbled that Nelson's turning out of the battle line was an unauthorized departure from the Admiral's prescribed plan of battle.

"It certainly was so," snapped Sir John, "and if ever you commit such a breach of your orders, I will forgive you also!" The remark cut Calder like a whip. He deserved it—but smoldering jealousy and resentment against Nelson burned within him. Strangely—but as so often happened before—Nelson was omitted from Admiral Jervis' official report to the Admiralty!

The sloop *Lively,* with Colonel Drinkwater on board, sailed to England with dispatches, and the first report of the battle. When he arrived, the gloom was as thick as a London fog.

News had reached England that the Spanish Fleet had sailed to join the French Fleet. The British people thought there was little hope of stopping them, and the invasion of England was expected at any moment. They had not yet heard of the victory off Cape St. Vincent.

Following years of dismal reports from the Continent and the Mediterranean, the good news burst through the gloom like sunshine! The official reports failed to tell of the interesting drama off Cape St. Vincent, but Colonel Drinkwater and the "fleet grapevine" supplied the colorful details.

Sir Gilbert Elliot had also observed the action from the decks of the *Lively*. "Nothing in the world was ever more noble than the transaction of the *Captain* from beginning to end," he enthusiastically wrote to Nelson. "The glorious group of your ship and her two prizes, fast in your grip, was never surpassed, and I dare say never will."

For years the sailors of the fleet regaled their friends with stories of Nelson off Cape St. Vincent on Valentine's Day, 1797. The audacity of boarding the larger 84-gun Spanish ship *San Nicolas*, when his own was a wreck, was colorful enough. But to use the decks of the captured *San Nicolas* to cross over and board the first-rate *San Josef* of 112 guns was unheard of! This unusual act was referred to around the fleet as "Nelson's patent bridge for boarding first-rates!"

The navy families were especially proud of the victory. From England, Fanny Nelson wrote:

"My anxiety was far beyond my powers of expression. Lady Saumarez came running to tell me she had letters from her husband (Captain James Saumarez of the *Orion*). He said, 'Commodore Nelson's conduct is above praise.' You are universally the subject of conversation.

"What can I attempt to say to you about boarding?" she scolded. "You have been most wonderfully protected—you have done desperate actions enough. Now may I, indeed I do, beg that you never board again. Leave it for Captains."

In honor of the victory, Admiral Jervis was given the title Earl of St. Vincent—Admiral William Parker, Baronet—Nelson, a Knight of the Bath, and shortly after the battle, he became Rear Admiral of the Blue. Gold medals were struck for all the captains and admirals involved in the battle.

The sword Nelson received from the fallen Spanish Rear Admiral Winthuysen was sent to the Corporation of Norwich to be displayed among the war trophies in the Guildhall.

"I know no place," Nelson wrote, "where it would give me or my family more pleasure to have it kept, than in the Capitol City of the County in which I had the honour to be born."

The Spanish Fleet had failed to rendezvous with the French. Instead, they had suffered a defeat, and had put into port at Cádiz—to repair their ships and bandage their wounded pride.

Now, the French, running wild with successes under the plundering Napoleon, were forced to delay their greedy dreams of invasion. Without Nelson's brilliant "disobedience," the Spanish might have broken through, joined the French, invaded England, and changed the course of history!

CHAPTER TEN

"I NEVER EXPECTED TO RETURN"

Two Spanish treasure ships were reported bound for Cádiz, and Nelson was chosen to intercept them. Sailing in the *Irresistible* on March 5 together with three other ships, he patrolled off the coast near Cádiz, without any sign of the gold-laden ships.

When the rest of the fleet joined him off Cádiz, Nelson shifted his pennant back to the patched-up *Captain.* Hearing of his promotion on April 1, he hoisted his blue admiral's flag for the first time.

General De Burgh had finally received his orders to evacuate Elba and the ships carrying his troops were now making their way toward Gibraltar. With no British Fleet presently in the Mediterranean, Nelson volunteered to meet them, and sailed on April 12 to escort the force safely to Gibraltar. When he rejoined the fleet, Nelson was given command of the inshore squadron blockading Cádiz.

In the spring of 1797, England and the Royal Navy were shocked by the mutinies of the Channel Fleet at Spithead and the Nore. One by one, the mutinous ships were sent to the Mediterranean Fleet, where Admiral Jervis, now Lord St. Vincent, would know how to deal with them.

"What do they mean," he grumbled, "by invariably sending me the mutinous ships? Do they think I will be the hangman of the fleet?"

St. Vincent disliked hanging, but since it had to be done, he favored quick and certain punishment. Four men from the *St. George* were convicted of mutiny and sentenced to death by hanging.

"The sentence must be carried into execution tomorrow morning," ordered St. Vincent, "although it is Sunday."

When Vice Admiral Thompson objected to violating the sabbath, he was sent back to England. Nelson, as always, supported St. Vincent.

"We know not what might have been hatched by a Sunday's grog—now your discipline is safe."

Nelson cared little what command he was given as long as he had the right sort of men to work with. His new flagship, however, was the worst ship of them all—the 74-gun *Theseus.*

St. Vincent called the ship "an abomination," but he promised the First Lord of the Admiralty that, "Nelson and Miller will soon put the *Theseus* to right."

When Nelson went aboard the *Theseus* at the end of May, he found the ship without supplies and in miserable condition. He promptly set out to correct the situation. Nelson was not sure whether he had a crew of scoundrels, or good men too long abused by an inept captain and a bully of a first lieutenant.

Captain Miller and a loyal group of "old *Agamem-*

nons" were transferred from the *Captain* to the *Theseus* as a stabilizing influence. In only two weeks, fair dealing and consideration for the crew produced results!

One hot night in June, during the mid-watch, a scrap of paper was dropped on the quarterdeck. It was a crudely-written note from the "Ship's Company." Taken down to the Admiral's cabin, it was read by the dim light of the lamp swinging from the overhead.

"Success attend Admiral Nelson! God bless Captain Miller! We thank them for the officers they have placed over us. We are happy and comfortable, and will shed every drop of blood in our veins to support them. The name of *Theseus* shall be immortalized as high as the *Captain*'s."

In those mutinous days, this note would have been an amazing gesture for any ship of the British Navy. Written by the crew, in the worst ship of all, it revealed the pride they felt toward their famous Admiral. Nelson's contagious spirit had "rubbed off" on every man on board.

It was not long before the crew would have a chance to "shed their blood to support" their new Admiral and Captain.

During the inshore blockade, Nelson ordered nighttime bombardments of Cádiz, and hoped that the raids would force the Spanish Fleet to sortie from port. On the night of July 3, the bomb ship *Thunderer* placed bombs within twenty-five hundred yards of the town walls. As the bombs exploded, the Spaniards sent out a swarm of armed launches. They soon clashed with the British barges, under the command of Nelson, Captain Miller, and Captain Fremantle of the *Seahorse.*

In the melee that followed, one of the Spanish launches, with twenty-six men aboard, banged against Nelson's barge. Nelson's ten men, brandishing cutlasses, grappled with the Spaniards in a hand-to-hand struggle.

As Nelson leaped into their launch, one of the Spaniards slashed at him with his heavy, curved sword. John Sykes, the coxswain of the barge, quickly jumped in front of Nelson, intercepted the blow, and saved Nelson's life.

After a fierce and bloody fight, the Spanish launch was captured. Eighteen of the Spanish crew were dead. Sykes, who had twice saved Nelson's life, spent several weeks in the sickbay of the *Theseus*, recovering from his painful wounds.

The promise given in the note dropped on the quarterdeck of the *Theseus* was being fulfilled. St. Vincent was delighted to hear how bravely the crew of "the worst ship of the fleet" had fought.

Nelson had very effectively blockaded Cádiz, and also made two bold attacks on the harbor at night in the hope of luring the Spanish Fleet out for battle. These raids served to consolidate the crew of the *Theseus* into a fighting band of loyal men. This was fortunate, for the *Theseus* was about to embark on an exciting and trying venture.

The British learned that one of the reported treasure ships, loaded with gold from Manila, had put into port at Teneriffe, Santa Cruz Island. The ship carried such a valuable cargo that it could not risk approaching a port of Spain during the tight British blockade. The cargo was therefore unloaded at Teneriffe.

Nelson and Captain Troubridge of the *Culloden* were put in charge of planning an attack on the Island. General De Burgh's 3,700 army troops, who had just evacuated Elba, were available. However, the General, as usual, would not cooperate, and Nelson was given 200 marines instead!

Special scaling ladders, guns, and ammunition were ordered, and every detail of the attack plan was carefully worked out. Nelson would command afloat, and Troubridge would serve as "the General" ashore. They pitched in enthusiastically on this new challenge.

Four ships-of-the-line set sail for the Canary Islands on the fifteenth of July. The *Theseus* led the way, followed by Captain Troubridge in the *Culloden*, Captain Hood in the *Zealous*, and Captain Fremantle in the *Seahorse.* Two frigates, the *Emerald* and *Terpsichore*, the cutter *Fox*, and a mortar boat rounded out the force.

Before sunset on July 20, the mountain peak of Teneriffe pierced the horizon sixty miles away. After dark, Troubridge approached with his landing parties. They embarked in the two frigates, not wanting the sails of their big ships-of-the-line to be seen.

It was planned first to take the fort near the town. Once it was in British hands, the ships-of-the-line could sail in after daybreak and completely control the town and port.

The contrary wind and current kept the two frigates far offshore all night. When dawn arrived, they still were not close to the Island. Thinking that the fort was alerted for a direct attack, Troubridge decided to seize a position above the fort. Instead of acting directly on his change of plan, he first wanted to clear it with Nelson in the *Theseus*. This proved a mistake—gone was the element of surprise.

Nelson approved the plan immediately, and Troubridge proceeded toward a landing. However, valuable time had been lost. The hours of delay had given the alarmed islanders plenty of time to prepare for the assault. The landing parties jumped ashore from the boats, but could make no advance against the stronger, well-positioned enemy.

The ships-of-the-line sailed close in to the shore to bombard the fort and batter it into submission. At the mercy of the brisk wind blowing against the ships, they could not gain a position close enough to bring their guns into range. As night fell, Troubridge reembarked his landing parties, who were far outnumbered by the enemy. Nelson recalled the frigates, and they joined the rest of the ships. For two days, the offshore winds made any further attack impossible.

The squadron had anchored three miles from the town, and on July 24, a night assault was decided upon. Nelson wanted to make one more all-out attempt.

That evening, Nelson had dinner in the *Seahorse*, with Captain Fremantle and his new bride, Betsy. At the dinner table, they tried to sound confident and pleasant in Betsy's presence, even though they had misgivings about the chances of success against a town and fort so thoroughly prepared.

During the evening, a thousand men climbed into the landing boats with scaling ladders, grappling irons, and guns. An hour before midnight they shoved off. It was a long, hard pull to the shore against the strong current and heavy surf. Some of the boats were tied together until they neared the breakwater.

Nelson felt that this attack was "a forlorn hope, yet the honor of our Country called for the attack, and that I should command it. I never expected to return."

As he went over the side, Nelson urged Lieutenant Josiah Nisbet, his stepson, not to go along. He did not want Fanny to lose both her husband and her son at the same time. Josiah, however, refused to stay on board the *Theseus*, and insisted upon joining him in his boat.

They drew away from the ship, and the men, tugging on the oars, headed toward the jetty. They were to charge ashore in a group, take the jetty by storm, and capture the batteries defending it. The cutter *Fox* was to follow the boats with supporting men, arms, and equipment.

Nelson approached the breakwater with a small group of boats. They were very close before they were noticed in the darkness. Suddenly, the silence was shattered by a flash and roar of guns. The men jumped out of the boats, and raced forward under a blistering fire.

Church bells in the town clanged in alarm as everyone ran for defense or for cover. Nelson's sailors and marines succeeded in spiking the enemy guns, but a withering fire opened up from the nearby houses, driving them back with heavy losses.

Nelson stepped out of his boat in the teeth of more than thirty booming guns. As he drew his sword, and stepped out of the boat, he was struck in the right arm. Grasping his sword with his left hand, he fell back, and was caught by Josiah. The young man quickly applied a tourniquet to Nelson's shattered arm with his neckerchief to stop the flow of blood, an action which probably saved his life. One of Nelson's men ripped off his shirt to make a sling.

The men nearby shoved the boat off, and headed back to the *Theseus*. They had just cast off, under the fire-belching guns, when a shell struck the *Fox* along the water line. The ship went down very quickly, drowning Lieutenant Gibson and ninety-seven of his crew.

Nelson ordered his boat to turn toward the men struggling in the water. He gave no thought to the risk of his bleeding to death, as he helped pull men out of the water with his left hand. They rescued the survivors, and headed back for the ship loaded down with the soaking wet men. All around in the water floated the remains of his overturned boats, telling Nelson of the disaster and failure, which he already suspected.

Finally, the boat came alongside one of the ships. Nelson recognized it as the *Seahorse*, and refused to go aboard.

"I had rather suffer death than alarm Mrs. Fremantle by her seeing me in this state, and when I can give her no tiding whatever of her husband."

The men then rowed the boat over to the *Theseus*. Here he refused the offer of a boatswain's chair, slung from the yardarm. After bobbing in the sea for over an hour in the boat with his arm bleeding and shattered, he insisted on climbing up the ship's side. On the deck, Midshipman Hoste later described Nelson's return.

"At two o'clock in the morning Admiral Nelson returned on board, being dreadfully wounded in the right arm with a grapeshot. I leave you to judge my situation when I beheld our boat approach with him —who I may say has been a second father to me. His right arm dangled by his side, while with the other he helped himself to jump over the ship's side.

"With a spirit that astonished everyone, he told the surgeon to get his instruments ready, for he knew he must lose his arm, and that the sooner it was off the better."

Nelson went below and "underwent the amputation," Hoste recalled, "with the same firmness and courage that have always marked his character."

The operation, performed on a mess table, was little better than skilled butchery. The surgical knives and saw applied to Nelson's arm were cold and unsterilized, and the surgical techniques of that time were pitifully inadequate. As the ship rolled at anchor, his arm was removed "very high near the shoulder" by the uncertain light of a swinging lantern.

Back ashore disaster mounted. In the darkness, many of the boats missed their intended landing at the jetty and found themselves at the mercy of the breakers to the left and right. Most of the boats which attempted to land through the heavy surf capsized, soaking the ammunition and casting adrift much of the equipment. As the surf rolled in, the flotsam and jetsam tumbled about in mocking futility.

Troubridge courageously gathered whatever men

he could and advanced through the town to the appointed rendezvous at the square. They were a motley collection of men—wet, bloody, hungry, and exhausted. Some had no guns, some carried muskets that would not fire, and others held pikes and cutlasses. They stood in the square despondently listening to the roar of the cannon near the beach where Nelson was struck and the *Fox* had sunk.

They waited about an hour for the force from the breakwater to join them. When they did not come, Troubridge sent a sergeant with two of the local townsmen to the fortress with a surrender ultimatum. For sheer "crust," this bluff has hardly been matched in military history! Troubridge was a leader trapped in a hostile square with a small number of men, carrying a sad assortment of weapons and ammunition that was well soaked with salt water!

Moreover, the entire group was separated from their support. Their only means of escape was by boats which were capsized or stove in—most of them long since carried off by the ocean current. Along with the splintered boats and oars, other vital equipment was at that same time tossing about on the waves off shore. Troubridge's men had scarcely a single piece of equipment with which to scale the walls of the citadel, nor a musket whose soggy ammunition would fire.

Captain Troubridge could hardly state the futility of his bluff more eloquently: "I fear the sergeant was shot on his way, as I heard nothing of him afterwards."

By dawn, Troubridge was joined in the square by Captain Hood and Captain Miller, whose boats had landed on the opposite side of the breakwater. The

British force now numbered about 350 men, with a small supply of dry ammunition captured from the Spanish. Of the group that succeeded in landing with Nelson, not one made it to the square!

Troubridge's position was ludicrously hopeless. He tried to get his rag-tag band in motion, but found "the streets commanded by field pieces, and upwards of 8,000 Spaniards and 100 French under arms, approaching by every avenue."

With no provisions, no word from Nelson, no hope for victory, there remained only the chance to escape with their lives. Troubridge finally had to admit the hopelessness of his predicament. With typical audacity he sent a flag of truce to the Governor, threatening to burn down the town, though reluctantly, unless his terms were met! He demanded that his men be permitted to return to the ships with their arms.

The audacity of Troubridge was more than matched by the chivalry of the Governor, Don Juan Gutiérrez. He not only granted Troubridge the privilege of withdrawing his men, but provided him with the captured British boats that were still usable! However, he did demand that no further assault be made on Teneriffe by the British. Prisoners were exchanged, and the local hospital offered to receive all the British wounded.

With the remainder of his men, Troubridge marched down to the jetty with colors flying! Embarking in their boats, they shoved off for the ships. The British remained anchored off Santa Cruz for three more days, taking on supplies from their gallant "enemies," and bringing aboard the wounded from the hospital.

To top it all off, the Governor gave Nelson two

casks of fine Canary Island wine. In return, Nelson sent ashore a quantity of English cheese and beer to show his appreciation! With this courtesy between victor and vanquished, Nelson hoisted the signal to get underway, leaving Santa Cruz and defeat behind.

In 1519—278 years before—Magellan had departed from Teneriffe on his voyage around the world. Now this obscure geographical landmark again made history as the place where Nelson suffered his only defeat, and lost his right arm.

Lord St. Vincent was deeply grieved over the loss of Nelson's arm. In a way, he too lost his "right arm," when Nelson departed for England. Captain Bowen of the *Terpsichore* had lost his life in the battle, and Captain Fremantle had returned to Betsy seriously wounded. Lord St. Vincent cast no blame on Nelson, for he knew that with such overwhelming odds success was not possible.

Nelson was in excruciating pain. Losing an arm in the year 1797 was a dangerous matter—prolonged infection and gangrene often resulted in death in this stage of medical artlessness. Also, Nelson's spirits were low, for he had little hope that the Royal Navy could use a one-armed Admiral.

"I am become a burden to my friends and useless to my country," Nelson scrawled in a left-handed note to Lord St. Vincent.

"When I leave your command I become dead to the world. I go hence, and am no more seen. You will excuse my scrawl, considering it is my first attempt."

Nelson did not realize that his greatest triumphs were still to come!

In August, Nelson took passage back to England

in the *Seahorse,* and Betsy Fremantle served as nurse for both her wounded husband and his Admiral. When the *Seahorse* anchored at Spithead on the first of September, Nelson left for Bath to recover from his wounds. There, his wife Fanny and his father joined him—for the first time in over four and a half years he was reunited with his family.

CHAPTER ELEVEN

"I WILL FIND THEM OUT —AND BRING THEM TO BATTLE"

In London, at the end of September, 1797, King George III presented Nelson with the impressive star of Knight of the Bath. This honor entitled him to his own coat of arms.

Nelson proved he was recovering his health and quick wit when, at the presentation ceremony, the King exclaimed: "You have lost your right arm!" and Nelson replied "But not my right hand, as I have the honor of presenting Captain Berry to your Majesty."

In December, Nelson wrote to the Duke of Clarence: "Not a scrap of that ardour with which I have hitherto served our King has been shot away."

It was not long before the Admiralty granted Nelson another ship, the 74-gun *Vanguard.* His request for Captain Edward Berry as the ship's commanding officer was gladly granted. At Spithead, his blue admiral's pennant was hoisted in the *Vanguard* on March 29, 1798. By the tenth of April, with the shores of England disappearing astern, the *Vanguard* headed for Nelson's happy hunting ground—the Mediterranean.

"I am very happy to send you Sir Horatio Nelson again," Lord Spencer, the First Lord of the Admiralty wrote to Lord St. Vincent, "not only because I believe I cannot send you a more zealous, active, and approved officer, but because I have reason to believe that his being under your command will be agreeable to your wishes."

During Nelson's absence in England, Lord St. Vincent had experienced difficult times. He suffered from the usual lack of supplies, the constant threat of an overwhelming force of Spanish and French ships, and an added threat of mutiny in his own fleet. After months of staggering reversals, the Commander-in-chief was delighted to hear of Nelson's return.

"The arrival of Admiral Nelson has given me new life," he penned to Lord Spencer. "You could not have gratified me more than in sending him.

"His presence in the Mediterranean is so very essential that I mean to put the *Orion* and *Alexander* under his command, with the addition of three or four frigates, and send him away to endeavor to ascertain the real object of the preparations made by the French."

It was clear that Lord St. Vincent had other plans for Nelson than to join the fleet in the blockade of Cádiz. At the end of April, two days after he had welcomed him back off Cádiz, he sent Nelson into the Mediterranean.

"The appearance of a British squadron in the Mediterranean," Lord Spencer had advised, "is a condition on which the fate of Europe may at this moment depend."

Nelson's squadron set off in high spirits with the "fate of Europe" in its trust. A huge armada was fitting out in ports of France and Italy. Great preparations, particularly at Toulon, had been made for an invasion force. Where Napoleon was going to invade, and what he was going to seize, was unknown. It would be Nelson's job to find out.

Entering the Mediterranean on the eighth of May, Nelson again sailed through the Pillars of Hercules, and watched the Rock of Gibraltar disappear astern. His high spirits were soon dampened, however. A violent gale struck his squadron on the twentieth, toppling the main and mizzen topmasts of the *Vanguard.* The foremast snapped close to the deck, and the proud *Vanguard* was taken in tow by the *Alexander*, under Captain Alexander Ball.

While heading down the coast of Sardinia to reach a port for repairs, heavy ground swells carried the ships toward the rocky shore. The light winds were of little help, and the *Vanguard* almost landed on the rocks. Captain Ball persistently refused to leave the *Vanguard* behind, and narrowly squeeked past the danger. The ships anchored safely at the southern tip of Sardinia on the twenty-third, where the sailors worked like Trojans to repair the *Vanguard* and make her ready for sea.

The gale was unlucky in other ways. It carried the French Fleet eastward out of Toulon, and down the Italian coast toward Africa. In the meantime, the storm had separated Nelson's frigates from the ships-of-the-line. The commodore of his frigate division, Captain George Hope, decided the *Vanguard* was so badly smashed that she had to sail to Gibraltar for repairs. He therefore set course for Gibraltar.

Nelson set out to meet the frigates at the appointed rendezvous, but they did not appear. However, on the morning of June fifth, the brig *Mutine*, under Captain Thomas Hardy, arrived with important news. Nelson's mission had been expanded—he was to "take, burn, sink or destroy" the armada of ships bearing Napoleon's invasion force!

To accomplish this, Nelson's detached squadron was being enlarged to fleet size. Nelson waited for his additional ships-of-the-line, and for his badly needed frigates. Frigates were the "eyes" of his fleet, and his immediate task was to search for the French. Unfortunately, his frigates never did appear.

While Nelson searched in vain for the French armada, a battle over his appointment to command the detached fleet was raging. Two of the senior rear admirals, Admiral Parker and Admiral Orde, who were jealous of the preference shown Nelson, would not have been too unhappy if Nelson's mission failed.

"I naturally expected to be sent," Sir William Parker wrote from the *Prince George*, "but the ships separated without any notice being taken of me, to be under the command of an officer [Nelson] very much my junior. This must necessarily be considered a doubt of my abilities or worse. I feel it the most injurious conduct toward me, and the most serious attack upon my reputation as an officer."

His letters to the Admiralty and Lord St. Vincent continued to "boil over" with indignation. He finally requested to be removed from Lord St. Vincent's command. This request was granted, with pleasure!

However meddlesome Parker may have been, he more than met his match in the "complaint department" in Admiral Sir John Orde, sailing in the *Princess Royal.* Orde carried on a daily barrage of sharp and bitter letters in protest over Lord St. Vincent's choice of Nelson.

"My Lords," Orde wrote to the Admiralty, "Sir Horatio Nelson, a junior officer and just arrived from England, is detached from the Mediterranean Fleet with the command of twelve sail-of-the-line. I must not say I am surprised at this measure, but I cannot conceal from your Lordships how much I feel hurt."

Lord St. Vincent finally ran completely out of patience with Sir John Orde. Already overburdened with more important matters than seniority numbers and wounded pride, he asked Orde to stop writing so many annoying letters. When Orde would not stop, St. Vincent ordered him to haul down his flag in the *Princess Royal*, and embark in the *Blenheim* for return to England.

"Rear Admiral Sir John Orde, having very much annoyed and interrupted me in the discharge of my duty, by attempts to force me into a correspondence of a nature highly derogatory to discipline, I have directed that Admiral to proceed to England, as per enclosed order."

Orde returned to England, but wanted revenge for his wounded vanity.

"I request their Lordships of the Admiralty to order a court-martial to try the Earl of St. Vincent, for treating me in a manner injurious to my credit and character."

Admiral Orde's constant needling with his pen resulted in the undermining of his own career. The witnesses he had planned to use from the fleet decided to remain with Lord St. Vincent in the Mediterranean. When the court-martial fell through, Orde published his own biased version of the story.

The "last straw" in Orde's battle was to challenge the sick and aging Lord St. Vincent to a duel! This sealed whatever future he had in the wax of his own bitterness. King George III finally stepped in, and wrote a letter to the Admiralty.

"Sir John Orde has been so absurd as to turn into a personal affront, what was only his commanding officer's employing that discretional power which his station authorized."

Consequently, Orde walked the gangplank of public disapproval, and dropped into the sea of oblivion.

It was unknown to Nelson at this time that he was acquiring these two enemies. However, even if he had known, that would have been the least of his worries. He had more important matters on his mind.

The puzzling search for the French Fleet began on the seventh of June. It led Nelson to Naples by the seventeenth, where no information could be gained, although his ships were able to load a few supplies there.

Nelson guessed that the French armada had sailed for Alexandria, Egypt. To find out for certain would require a long voyage to the eastern Mediterranean. This would be dangerous, for it would widely separate the two British Fleets. So divided, the British Fleet would be badly outnumbered by enemy ships.

Still, the long cruise to Egypt would either solve the problem of finding the French, or it would prove an embarrassing "wild-goose" chase. Captain Thomas Troubridge had joined him with ten 74-gun ships-of-the-line and the 50-gun *Leander*. Without delay, they set sail for Alexandria with fourteen ships-of-the-line. Lord St. Vincent had given Nelson his head, and certainly enough rope to hang it with!

As they headed for Alexandria, the British and French Fleets passed just out of sight of each other on June 21! Three French frigates were sighted, and the *Leander* was signaled to pursue them. Nelson decided not to risk separating his force, however, and recalled the *Leander* before she got out of sight.

It is possible that this recall affected the history of Europe! Over the horizon, still out of sight of the *Leander*, was the enormous armada of the French Fleet, and with it were Napoleon's troop transports! The French frigates were actually their outer screen. If Nelson had sighted the fleet and troop ships, a decisive battle would have been fought then and there. As fate would have it, Napoleon's forces had the good luck to pass unseen. For seventeen years Bonaparte was to keep Europe in turmoil, instead of meeting his "Waterloo" by Nelson's hand at sea!

That night the French and British ships passed so close to each other than Admiral de Brueys, on board *L'Orient*, could hear the minute guns of the British firing across the haze-covered water. At dawn, the horizon was clear of any French ships, and Nelson's frustrating search continued.

Day after day they scanned the empty horizon for sight of a French sail. Increasingly, Nelson regretted the lack of frigates to do his scouting.

"We are crowding sail for Alexandria," Captain

Saumarez wrote from the *Orion*. "At present it is very doubtful whether we shall fall in with the French at all, as we are proceeding upon the merest conjecture only, and not on any positive information.

"Some days must now elapse before we can be relieved from our cruel suspense. If, at the end of our journey, we find we are upon a wrong scent, our embarrassment will be great indeed. Did the chief responsibility rest with me, I fear it would be more than my too irritable nerves would bear."

By June 26, Nelson drew within 250 miles of Alexandria, and sent the brig *Mutine* ahead to seek out information. Hardy reported that there were no French ships at Alexandria. Nelson did not realize that he had arrived before the French! As a result they sailed away in further search.

To an observer looking out at sea from the Pharos Tower at Alexandria, the sails of Nelson's ships would have hardly dipped below the horizon to the northeast, when the masts of Napoleon's armada pierced the horizon to the northwest!

Had Nelson waited a short while, or sailed in a different direction from Alexandria, the search would have been over. Fate had stepped in again! If it had happened otherwise, Napoleon's loaded troop transports would doubtless have been annihilated at sea—perhaps with Napoleon himself!

Badly in need of water and supplies, the British ships sailed to Syracuse, Sicily, arriving there on the nineteenth of July. Nelson lamented that he was "as ignorant of the situation of the enemy as I was twenty-seven days ago.

"Every moment I have to regret the frigates having left me," he wrote to St. Vincent. "But if the French are above water, I will find them out, and if possible bring them to battle. You have done your part in giving me so fine a fleet, and I hope to do mine in making use of them."

Anchors were hoisted and sails unfurled on July 25, and Nelson set his course eastward again for Alexandria. Three days later, a Greek fisherman reported that a month before he had seen a fleet sailing eastward. It was "so large that the ships spread far over the horizon."

Unfortunately, the French Fleet had arrived at Alexandria, and Napoleon had already disembarked his troops and supplies. His transport ships had been sent back to France, but the fleet remained.

During the search for the French Fleet, Nelson's captains frequently boarded his flagship for conferences. On the *Vanguard*, every possible battle formation and condition under which they might meet the French was reviewed. There was not a captain who did not know exactly what to do, and how the Admiral wanted it done. When the time came there would be little need for last-minute communication, and hence no delay.

At 2:30 in the afternoon on August 1, a lookout in the masthead of the *Zealous* shouted down to the deck that he had sighted French ships at anchor in Aboukir Bay! Silt from the delta of the Nile had prevented their anchoring at Alexandria, fifteen miles to the west. The thirteen French ships-of-the-line were in a crescent-shaped formation near the shore, with four frigates nearby.

When Admiral de Brueys, in his flagship *L'Orient*,

heard the reports that the British were in sight, and moving toward the bay, he was not too alarmed. Night was falling, and the navigation hazards of the uncharted waters of the bay would certainly prevent them from risking an immediate attack. But, the French Admiral was wrong!

After being tormented by almost two months of agonizing search, Nelson did not hesitate a moment. Signals were hoisted to prepare for battle, and to form a single-column line.

These signals sent all hands aloft and scurrying about the decks. Bulkheads were removed on the gun decks to open the way for gun crews and ammunition passers. Tubs of water were placed alongside the guns to cool off the crews and douse fires. All loose furniture was secured. Galley fires were extinguished, and livestock were tied firmly. The decks were sprinkled with sand to prevent fires, and to keep the men from losing their footing in the slippery blood.

Topsides, the sails were rolled tightly and doused with water so they would not catch fire. Hammocks were brought up from below, and stowed along the weather deck nettings, to protect the crew from flying splinters and small-arms fire. Marines were stationed around the quarterdeck and aloft to fire at the French sharpshooters.

Powder passers took their places belowdecks deep within the holds of all ships-of-the-line. They worked in the dim light of rows of candles set within narrow, tin-lined gratings to guard against accidentally igniting the powder. Black handkerchiefs were tied around the gunners' ears to muffle the sound of the ship's guns.

With only a crude map of Aboukir Bay to guide them, ten British ships-of-the-line sailed in for the initial attack. Four of their ships were still miles away. As they approached the entrance to the bay, Nelson hailed Captain Samuel Hood of the *Zealous*. Uncertain of the shoals, Nelson ordered him to precede and take constant soundings to make sure the other ships did not run aground.

The signal for close action was hoisted at 5:40, and the line sailed in to attack. Captain Thomas Foley, in the *Goliath*, led the battle line. As he approached the first ship of the French line, the sun was going down, casting a reddish glow over the sky and the sea.

Foley took the initiative and acted on his own judgment, as Nelson had encouraged his captains to do. He decided that if the French ships were anchored only by the bow, there must be enough room between them and the shore to swing around their anchors without grounding. Therefore, he felt sure there would be room for the *Goliath*, and he boldly steered her to the shore-side of the French line.

This maneuver caught the French by surprise! It was so daring and unexpected that the French had not opened the shore-side gun ports to run out their cannon. Instead, they had all the mess tables, benches, and loose deck gear piled around their port-side batteries!

Nelson placed the *Vanguard* sixth in line to better control his ships from the middle. He watched his next four 74-gun ships, *Zealous*, *Orion*, *Theseus*, and *Audacious*, follow the *Goliath* into positions on the shore-side of the French line.

When Foley ordered the anchor dropped, it hung

up briefly and the *Goliath* drifted past the first French ship, the 74-gun *Le Guerrier*. By the time his anchor dug in and held, he was almost past the second ship, *Le Conquerant*.

Captain Hood brought the *Zealous* across the port bow of the *Le Guerrier*. At this instant, the first flash of fire leaped out of the French cannon and resounded across the bay. This signaled the beginning of the famous Battle of the Nile!

Their guns primed and doubled-loaded, the *Zealous* and *Goliath* answered the French fire with crushing success. In less than fifteen minutes, all the masts of *Le Guerrier* came crashing down in splinters, bringing with them a huge tangle of rigging, sails, and spars.

Le Conquerant fared no better. The flash and roar of guns from *Goliath* and *Audacious* (Captain Davidge Gould) ripped into her. She was the first to strike her colors.

Captain James Saumarez in the *Orion* passed the *Zealous* and *Goliath*, and anchored between the fifth and sixth French ships, the 74-gun *Le Peuple Souverain* and the 80-gun *Le Franklin*. The last to follow inside the line was Captain Ralph Miller in the *Theseus*. As he passed each French ship, he blasted it with a broadside. The British tars from the other ships cheered him on.

Some of the men had their wives on board (when permitted by the captain). A seaman in the *Goliath* saw little of the action, though he described his experiences belowdecks.

"Any of the information we got was from the boys and women who carried powder. In the heat of the action a shot came right through the magazine, but the carpenters plugged it, and stopped the water that was rushing in.

"I was much indebted to the gunner's wife who gave her husband and me a drink of wine every now and then, which lessened our fatigue much. There were some of the women wounded, and one woman died of her wounds."

In the *Orion*, Nancy Perriam assisted the surgeon with the wounded. She later told about a young boy whose arm had been pulled from the socket: "The boy bore the operation without a murmur, and when it was over he turned to me and said: 'Have I not borne it like a man?' Having said this, he immediately expired."

Nelson had Captain Berry bring the *Vanguard* along the seaward side of the French line, and anchored very close to the 74-gun *Le Spartiate*, third in the line.

"No colors were hoisted nor a gun fired," Berry wrote later, "until our van ships were within half gun shot. At this time the necessary number of our men were employed aloft in furling sail and on deck, in hauling the braces preparatory to our casting anchor. As soon as this took place, a most animated fire was opened from the *Vanguard*."

Captain Thomas Louis in the *Minotaur* and Captain John Peyton in the *Defence* followed the *Vanguard* on the outside of the line, and anchored near the fourth and fifth ships of the French. Their fire was concentrated on the 74-gun *L'Aquilon* and *Le Peuple Souverain*.

Captain Henry Darby brought the *Bellerophon*

through the flickering smoke of battle toward *Le Franklin*, which was sixth in line. Unfortunately, he missed by one ship, and anchored next to the huge French flagship, *L'Orient* of 120 guns!

No other ships were engaged with *L'Orient* at this time, and the *Bellerophon* fired valiantly but with about half the number of guns! After a spirited stand, she was completely overwhelmed by the guns of *L'Orient*, and was hammered out of position. Her masts were blasted into mere stumps. Her casualties were the highest of the British ships—200 of her 590 men were killed or wounded.

The *Majestic*, under Captain Westcott, fared little better. Her jibboom needled into the rigging of the 74-gun *L'Heureux*, where she was hung up temporarily and unable to maneuver. Before she worked her way free, Captain Westcott was killed. When the *Majestic* finally anchored, she was alongside the 80-gun *Le Tonnant*. In the blistering exchange of fire, *Majestic* suffered the second highest casualties of the British ships. *Le Tonnant*, with her masts smashed, struck her colors. She slipped her anchor cable, and drifted far behind the line to avoid the impending explosion of *L'Orient*.

Captain Thomas Troubridge in the *Culloden* had captured a French wine brig, and with his prize under tow, had fallen far astern when the battle started. Nelson had signaled him to drop his prize and join the fleet. In his anxiety to get into the battle, Troubridge turned too soon into the unfamiliar bay, and ran hard aground on a shoal. His chagrin at watching the battle while helplessly grounded was beyond words! However, he did save the *Swiftsure, Alex-*

ander, and *Leander* from running aground, by waving them off the shoal as they entered the bay.

The late arrivals, approaching after dark, had been miles away on scouting duty. Captain Benjamin Hallowell in the *Swiftsure* anchored between the *Le Franklin* and *L'Orient*. The *Alexander* sailed through the line and took position off the stern of *L'Orient*. Captain Thomas Thompson in the *Leander* neatly picked his way through smoke and gun flashes to anchor ahead of *Le Franklin*. She opened a raking fire on both *Le Franklin* and *L'Orient* beyond.

Nelson was watching the progress of the battle through the smoke and flash of firing. Suddenly, he was struck on the forehead by a piece of flying metal. As he fell to the deck, Captain Berry caught him. His forehead was laid open, and a fold of loose skin covered his one good eye.

Blinded and bleeding profusely, Nelson was led down to the surgeon in the ship's cockpit. He refused immediate attention, and waited for his turn with the rest of the wounded. After he was bandaged, he was told to lie down and rest; but rest was impossible with the guns thundering all around him.

About 9:15 on that memorable night, the greatest catastrophe of the entire battle occurred. A fire broke out on the poop deck of *L'Orient*. Before it could be extinguished, the blaze leaped and crackled up the rigging. Buckets of paint, brushes, and rags had not been cleared away, and these added to the fury of the fire. Captain Berry hurried below to report this development to Nelson. Nothing could keep him belowdecks now!

The fire spread quickly over the topside and

rigging of the big French ship. Other ships nearby slipped their cables to clear out, knowing that an explosion threatened at any moment. Suddenly, *L'Orient* erupted with an awesome roar and a huge burst of flame—brightly illuminating the whole battle scene. The stunning concussion was followed by a death-like silence, as all guns on both sides stopped firing.

The debris, blown high into the sky, started falling down all around the bay. Disappearing in the explosion were millions of dollars in gold, a large loot of stolen treasure from the Island of Malta, three tons of silver and gold plate, life-sized statues of the twelve apostles made of solid silver, and other valuable trophies of Napoleon's greed.

From the shore, the Arabs had lined up to watch the show illuminated by the light of the gun flashes and flames. They had just seen the climax of the battle. Nelson's first concern was to save *L'Orient*'s survivors, and he ordered the *Vanguard*'s only sound boat into the water to rescue them.

Before the French flagship blew up, Admiral de Brueys had already been killed. Struck in the head and twice in the body, he was propped in an armchair on deck, when a fourth shot cut him in two. Other high-ranking officers were also badly wounded. The captain of *Le Tonnant*, with a leg shattered and both arms wounded, sat in a tub of bran to prop him up and soak up the blood. From there, he directed the fighting of his ship until he bled to death. Nearly all of the French admirals and captains engaged in the battle were either killed or badly wounded.

The French ships had put up a blistering fight, but

they were no match for the British. The victors, too, had many killed and wounded. Captains Hood, Saumarez, Miller, and Ball were all seriously wounded, and Captain Westcott of the *Majestic* was killed.

When dawn broke over Aboukir Bay, the first six ships in the French line had surrendered. *L'Orient* had disappeared completely! *Le Tonnant*, though dismasted, had drifted back a mile from her former position. The next two French ships, *L'Heureux* and *Le Mercure*, had cast loose from their moorings to avoid the explosion. Both had run helplessly aground.

The last three ships, *Le Guillaume Tell*, *Le Genereux*, and *Le Timoleon*, still intact, tried to escape. However, when *Le Timoleon* ran aground, the ship's crew escaped to the shore and the captain set the ship on fire. The frigate *Le Sérieuse* had been sunk by a broadside from the *Orion*. Another, *L'Artemise*, had been set aflame by her captain.

Le Genereux and *Le Guillaume Tell*, with the frigates *La Diane* and *La Justice*, escaped to sea under the command of Rear Admiral Villeneuve. The *Zealous* was the only ship with sound enough rigging to pursue them. Nelson, seeing that the *Zealous* could not be supported, recalled her.

Nelson was a man who thought in terms of total victory. When he saw the two ships escaping, he was not completely satisfied with the greatest victory the British Navy had ever won!

After fighting all night, the men were so exhausted they fell asleep on their feet. Captain Miller in the *Theseus* reported his men "were so extremely jaded that as soon as they had hove our sheet anchor up, they dropped under the capstan-bars and were asleep in a moment in every sort of posture." When orders were given there were few who had the strength to carry them out.

All around there were ships without masts, shredded sails, and tangled rigging. In the water was the horrible evidence of death and destruction. The charred wreckage of *L'Orient* floated away, along with the dead bodies and other debris of battle.

It had been a hard-won victory. Nelson penned a letter to Lord St. Vincent: "My Lord, Almighty God has blessed His Majesty's Arms in the late Battle, by a great victory over the Fleet of the enemy, whom I attacked at sunset on the first of August, off the mouth of the Nile.

"The enemy were moored in a strong line of battle for defending the entrance of the Bay, flanked by numerous gun-boats, four frigates and a battery of guns and mortars on an island in their van—but nothing could withstand the squadron your Lordship did me the honor to place under my command.

"Their high state of discipline is well-known to you, and with the judgment of the captains, together with their valor, and that of the officers and men of every description, it was absolutely irresistible. Could anything from my pen add to the character of the captains I would write it with pleasure, but that is impossible."

With his throbbing head wound, Nelson was left with the wreckage of battle to organize and repair as best he could in the tropical summer heat.

Victory had been gained without losing a single British ship, although they had "only two masts standing out of nine sails-of-the-line." The enemy had lost 11 of their 13 ships-of-the-line, and more than 5,200 men.

Thus the greatest naval victory in British history had been won by the British, under the command of the illustrious Admiral Nelson. It was two months before any news of the victory reached England—two months during which "the fate of Europe" was not known.

CHAPTER TWELVE

"NAPLES IS A DANGEROUS PLACE"

With Nelson's victory at the Nile, Napoleon's dreams of an eastern empire were smashed, his fleet destroyed, and his domination in the Mediterranean ended. His army ashore was hemmed in by desert on three sides, and by a hostile fleet on the fourth. Supplies by sea were cut off, and escape back to France would be difficult without a French Fleet.

Nelson's ships, battered as they were, reigned supreme in the Mediterranean. Telling the world about the defeat of the French would be difficult. Nelson's frigates had never arrived, and thus he had been deprived of the "eyes" of his fleet. Now he needed the frigates for fast-sailing dispatch carriers.

Therefore, Captain Berry of the *Vanguard* was sent with dispatches in the *Leander*, with Captain Thompson. One set was addressed to Lord St. Vincent, and the other to the Admiralty.

The "patched up" *Leander* set sail on the sixth of August for her voyage to the fleet anchorage at Gibraltar. As the eighteenth dawned, the *Leander* sighted a sail near Crete. It was a French sail—that of the powerful and undamaged *Le Genereux*!

Captain Thompson knew his crippled 50-gun *Leander* was no match for the larger 80-gun *Le Genereux*. Besides, his crew was eighty men short, and the decks were loaded with the wounded from the Nile. He set sail to escape action, but *Le Genereux* had the wind in her favor and bore down on the hapless *Leander*.

By eight o'clock in the morning they were within gun range, and Thompson "commenced a vigorous cannonade on him." By 10:30, the two ships stood off at close range and pounded each other for five hours.

At 3:30 in the afternoon, the *Leander* was a wreck. Her masts were shot away, her hull shattered, and a third of her crew were battle casualties. Captain Thompson was wounded four times before he was forced to strike his colors to *Le Genereux*.

It had been a furious battle. The *Leander* had made a gallant stand. Although the French had won, there was little glory in defeating a smaller, crippled ship, loaded with wounded.

Unlike the British consideration for the wounded at the Nile, the treatment of prisoners and wounded by *Le Genereux*'s crew was disgraceful. Like a band of pirates, they stole everything they could lay their hands on. Captain Berry lost all his uniforms, and did not even have a pair of breeches to preserve his dignity!

"I had not a second coat," he wrote to Nelson, "and would have been literally 'sans culotte' had not Captain Thompson furnished me with that necessary article."

Thompson complained to Captain le Joille of *Le Genereux* over the theft of a miniature painting of his mother.

"I am sorry for it," the French captain replied icily, "but the fact is the French are expert at plunder."

In their haste to grab loot, the French trampled all over the wounded British sailors, causing excrutiating pain, and reopening bandaged wounds. A British surgeon's instruments were stolen from him while he was operating—amputating shattered arms and legs. The French crew proved themselves no better than the plundering legions of Napoleon's land forces. The British had a score to settle with *Le Genereux*.

After they had suffered much misery, Berry and Thompson were finally released and returned to England. The *Leander* was later recaptured at Corfu when Russian and Turkish forces defeated the French there in March, 1799. She was then returned to Great Britain.

With the forethought of a good seaman, Nelson sent a second ship with dispatches. Since his badly needed frigates still had not appeared, he sent the brig *Mutine*, under Captain Thomas Capel, to Naples. From there, Capel was to go by land up the boot of Italy, through Germany, and deliver the official news directly to the Admiralty.

On the first of September, the *Mutine* dropped anchor in the Bay of Naples. Captain Capel set out by land, and Lieutenant Hoste was ordered to take command of the ship.

Upon hearing the news of the British victory at the Nile, the Court at Naples went wild with joy. Lady Hamilton insisted that Capel and Hoste climb into her carriage and, to the clatter of horses' hoofs, she paraded them all over town. She wore a ribbon around her head inscribed "Nelson and Victory." Shouts of "Viva Nelson!" from the grinning mobs greeted them as they rode through the streets.

"You have no idea of the rejoicings that were made throughout Naples," wrote Lieutenant Hoste. "Bonfires and illuminations all over the town—it would require an abler pen than I am master of, to give you any account of."

Captain Saumarez sailed from Aboukir Bay to Gibraltar on the fourteenth of August with seven British ships and six French ships taken as prizes. Three of the French ships were such wrecks that they were burned.

On the nineteenth, Nelson set course for Naples with three ships, the *Vanguard*, *Alexander*, and *Culloden.* They were in horrible condition. To make her seaworthy, the *Culloden* had a sail wrapped under her hull to keep the water from rushing into her leaky bottom! The crew had to man the pumps during the entire voyage.

The faint and fitfull summer breezes pushed the three cripples slowly toward Naples in a voyage which took over a month. Ironically, Nelson's frigates showed up frequently during the cruise, now that there was little need for them. The slow passage, however, did give Nelson's wounded head some chance to mend.

"My head is ready to split," he wrote to Lord St. Vincent. "If there be no fracture, my head is severely shaken."

When Lady Hamilton and the Queen of Naples

Lord Nelson, *a painting by Lemuel F. Abbott. Nelson's uniform is decorated with the star of Knight of the Bath. The gold medal was presented by the King after the Battle of Cape St. Vincent. Engraved by T. Johnson.* (LIBRARY OF CONGRESS)

Naval scenes of Nelson's time. Above, The Embarkation. *Below,* The Fleet Getting Under Way. (BOTH, COURTESY OF THE ILLUSTRATED LONDON NEWS AND LIBRARY OF CONGRESS)

Above: HMS Agamemnon. *W. I. Pocock from a painting by N. Pocock.* (NATIONAL MARITIME MUSEUM)

Right: Boarding the San Josef, *by Bromley and Worthington. Commodore Nelson receives the sword of the Spanish admiral at the Battle of Cape St. Vincent.* (LIBRARY OF CONGRESS)

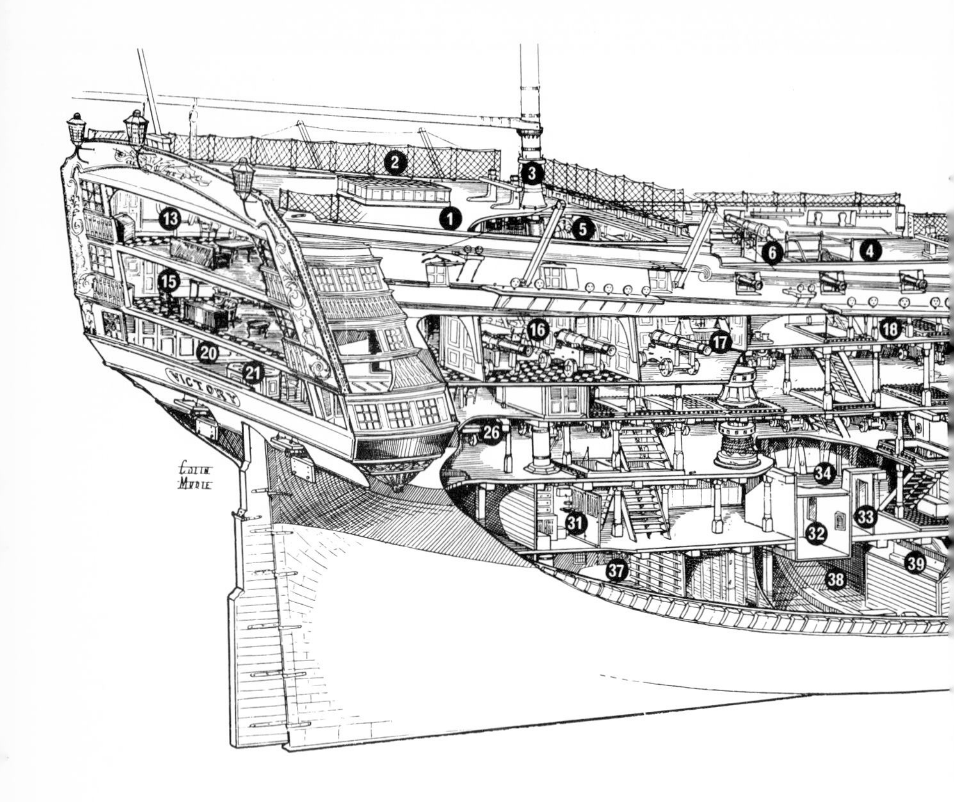

H.M.S. VICTORY AT THE TIME OF TRAFALGAR

The VICTORY was built to the design of Sir Thomas Slade. Her keel was laid down at the Old Single Dock, Chatham, on 23rd July 1759, and she was launched on 7th May, 1765.

Key to Drawing

1 Poop
2 Hammock Nettings
3 Mizzenmast
4 Quarter Deck
5 Steering Wheels
6 Here Nelson Fell
7 Pikes
8 Mainmast
9 Gangway
10 Fo'c'sle
11 Carronades
12 Foremast

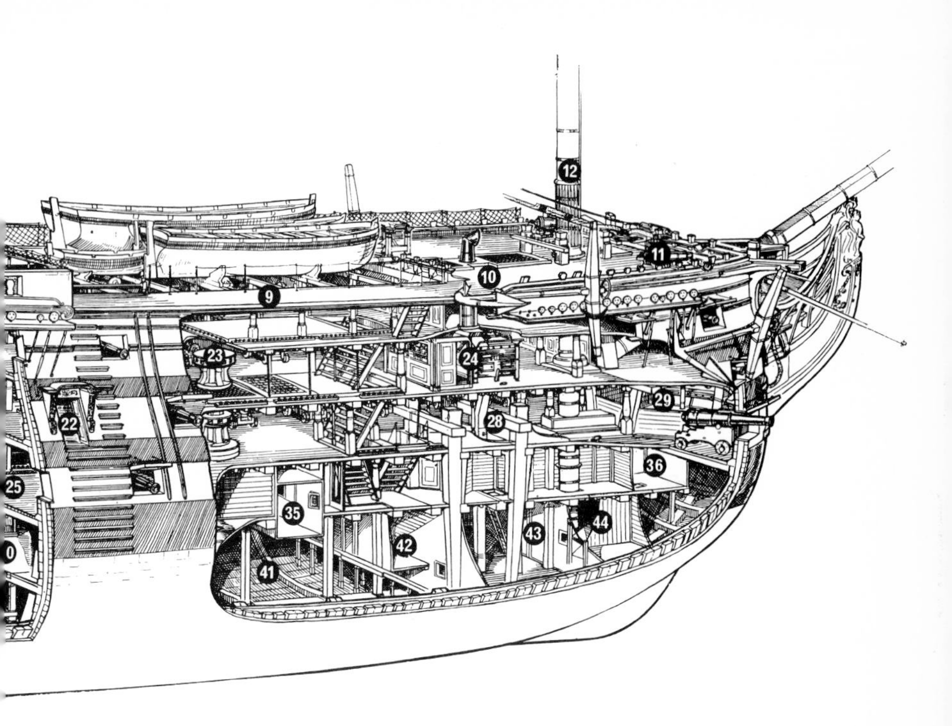

13 Captain Hardy's Cabin
14 Upper Deck
15 Nelson's Day Cabin
16 Nelson's Dining Cabin
17 Nelson's Sleeping Cabin with his cot
18 Shot Garlands
19 Middle Deck
20 Wardroom
21 Tiller Head
22 Entry Port
23 Capstan Head
24 Galley and Stove
25 Lower Deck
26 Tiller
27 Chain and Elm Tree Pumps
28 Mooring Bitts
29 Manger
30 Orlop
31 Sick Bay
32 Aft Hanging Magazine
33 Lamp Room
34 Midshipman's Berth—here Nelson died
35 Forward Hanging Magazine
36 Powder Store
37 Powder Room
38 Aft Hold
39 Shot Locker
40 Well
41 Main Hold
42 Cabin Store
43 Main Magazine
44 Filling Room

Armament

Lower Deck.......30 32-pounders
Middle Deck.......28 24-pounders
Upper Deck........30 12-pounders
Quarter Deck......12 12-pounders
Forecastle...........2 12-pounders
and 2 68-pounders
(Carronades)

Particulars

Length on Gun Deck.......186′ 0″
Length of Keel............151′ 0″
Moulded Breadth...........50′ 6″
Extreme Breadth...........51′ 10″
Depth in Hold.............21′ 6″
Displacement (approx.)..3,500 tons
Burthen...............2,162 tons

* * *

John Jervis, Earl of St. Vincent, *a painting by Hoppner. Engraved by H. Robinson.* (LIBRARY OF CONGRESS)

Encounter Off Cadiz, *by Bromley and Worthington. Engraving shows hand-to-hand fighting with swords and cutlasses during inshore blockade of Cadiz.* (LIBRARY OF CONGRESS)

Teneriffe, *by Bromley and Worthington. Nelson loses his arm during the attack.* (LIBRARY OF CONGRESS)

Horatio Nelson

Lord Nelson's Signature on being made a Lieutenant 11 April 1777.

Horatio Nelson

His ordinary writing before he lost his arm.

Horatio Nelson

His Signature 1. Sept. 1797 after the loss of his arm.

Bronte Nelson of the Nile

His Signature May 21. 1800.

Nelson & Bronte

His signature in the latter years of his life.

Nelson's signatures. (RARE BOOK COLLECTION, LIBRARY OF CONGRESS)

Lord Nelson's coat of arms. The crest is the San Josef. (NATIONAL MARITIME MUSEUM)

Battle of the Nile, *a painting by N. Pocock. The British squadron attacking the French Fleet on August 1, 1798, in Aboukir Bay.* (NATIONAL MARITIME MUSEUM)

Battle of the Nile, *a painting by Whitcombe. At right is French flagship* L'Orient *burning and about to explode.* (NATIONAL MARITIME MUSEUM)

Lady Hamilton, *a painting by George Romney.* (LIBRARY OF CONGRESS)

Battle of Copenhagen, *by Pocock and Kittoe. British ships sail in to attack the Danish line.* (NATIONAL MARITIME MUSEUM)

The First Journey of the HMS Victory. *Keel was laid down at the Old Single Dock, Chatham on July 23, 1759, and launched on May 7, 1765.* (LIBRARY OF CONGRESS)

The Last Journey of the HMS Victory. (LIBRARY OF CONGRESS)

HMS Victory. *The second row of windows were Nelson's quarters. Captain Hardy lived above. (Provided through the courtesy of the Commanding Officer of HMS* Victory, *and the* Victory *Museum)*

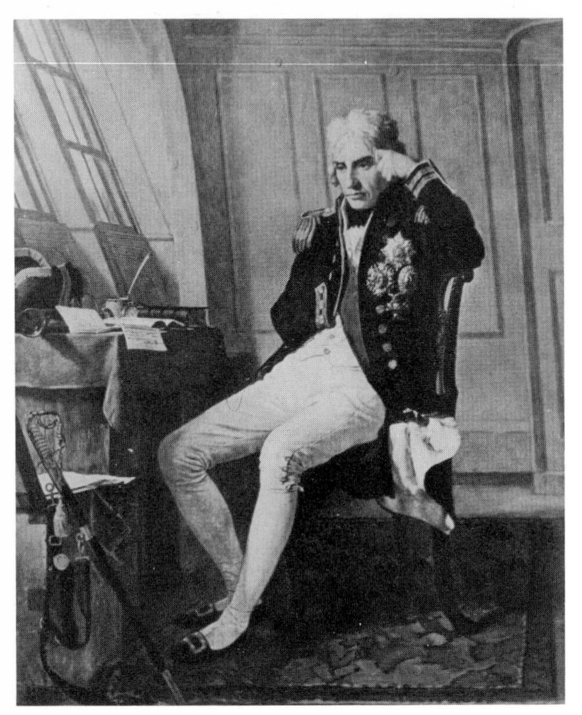

Lord Nelson in a thoughtful mood in his cabin aboard HMS Victory. (LIBRARY OF CONGRESS)

Sir Thomas Masterman Hardy, *a painting by R. Evans. Engraved by H. Robinson.* (LIBRARY OF CONGRESS)

Battle of Trafalgar, *a painting by Stansfield. HMS* Victory *closely engaged with French ships as the battle rages.* (NATIONAL MARITIME MUSEUM)

Death of Lord Nelson, *by J. L. G. Ferris. Nelson is wounded by a sharpshooter firing from the rigging of the* Redoubtable. (LIBRARY OF CONGRESS)

Anecdote at the Battle of Trafalgar, *an aquatint by M. Dourg after W. Heath. Jeannette Durand, wife of a crewman of the French ship* Achille, *is rescued after the ship, in background, has burned to the waterline.* (U.S. NAVY PHOTOGRAPH, COURTESY OF F. S. HICKS, NAVAL HISTORY DIVISION)

The principal ships in which Nelson served, from a painting by N. Pocock and engraved by Fittler. Left, Agamemnon *next to the* Captain. *Left center,* Vanguard. *Right,* Elephant *behind the* Victory. (NATIONAL MARITIME MUSEUM)

These Nelson medals were presented in April, 1845, in the Painted-hall, Greenwich Hospital, to the men who fought under the "immortal Nelson" at Cape St. Vincent, Teneriffe, Copenhagen, the Nile, and Trafalgar. (COURTESY, THE ILLUSTRATED LONDON NEWS AND LIBRARY OF CONGRESS)

HMS Collingwood, *sister ship to the* Vanguard. *She was named after Admiral Collingwood who, in the* Royal Sovereign, *broke through the enemy's line at Trafalgar.* (LIBRARY OF CONGRESS)

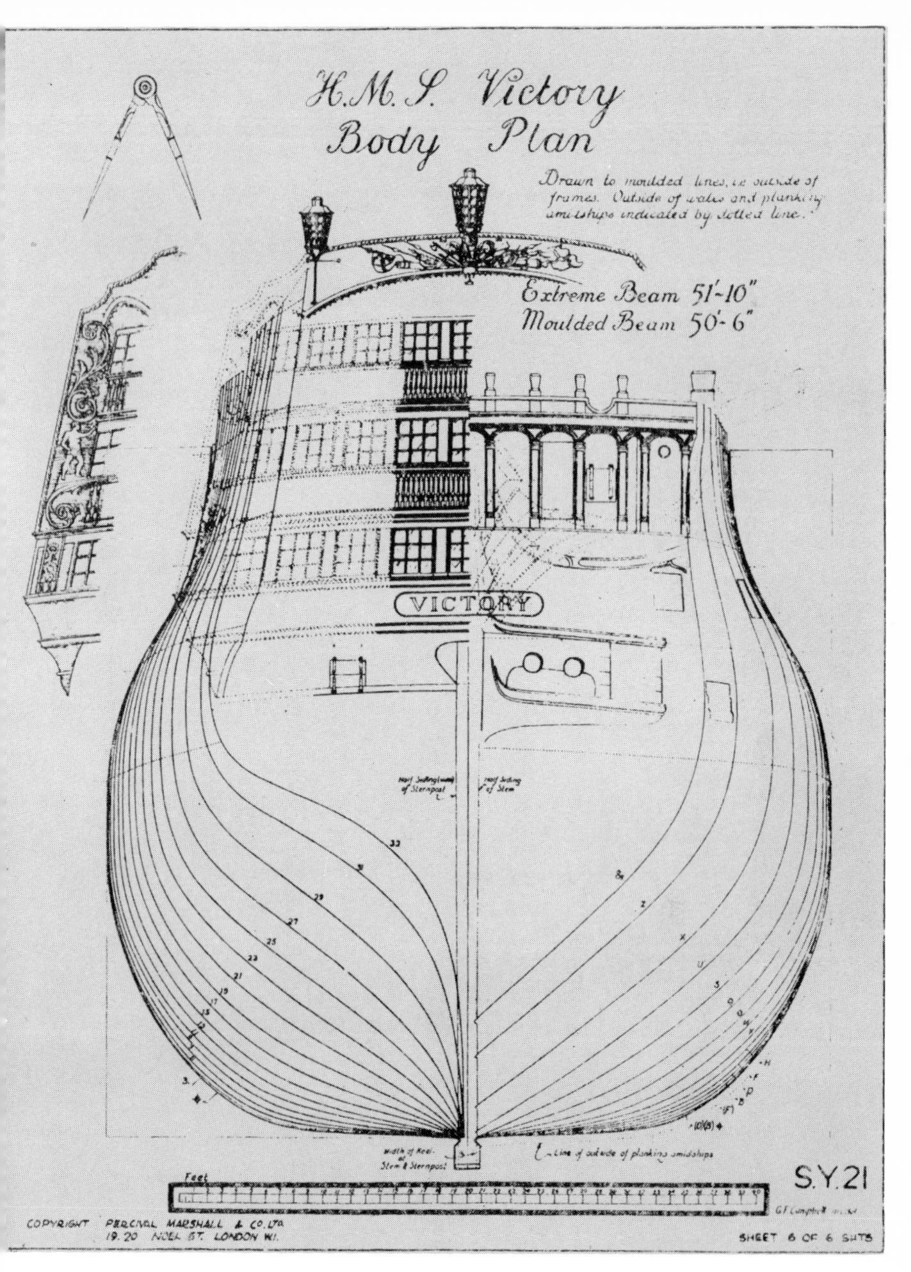

HMS Victory *body plan. (Provided through the courtesy of the Commanding Officer of HMS* Victory, *and the* Victory *Museum*)

HMS Victory. *The quarterdeck where Nelson fell. (Provided through the courtesy of the Commanding Officer of HMS* Victory*)*

Lower gundeck of the Victory. *(Provided through the courtesy of the Commanding Officer of HMS* Victory*)*

Lord Nelson, *a portrait in oils by Lemuel F. Abbott. The famous naval hero is shown here at the age of 43. In his hat, Nelson wears the "chelengk" set in diamonds, given to him by the Sultan of Turkey in honor of the victory of the Nile.* (NATIONAL MARITIME MUSEUM)

applied their feminine arts of flattery and praise, his head would soon be shaken even more!

The *Mutine* sailed from Naples in time to meet Nelson's ships off the Island of Stromboli on September 14. Lieutenant Hoste brought official correspondence and a letter from Lady Hamilton. The latter gave Nelson an idea of the hero's welcome he was about to receive!

"My dear, dear Sir," she wrote. "How shall I begin? What shall I say to you? 'Tis impossible I can write, for since last Monday I am delirious with joy, and assure you I have a fever caused by agitation and pleasure. God, what a victory!

"Never, never has there been anything half so glorious, so complete. I fainted when I heard the joyful news, and fell, and am hurt. But what of that? I should feel it a glory to die in such a cause. No, I would not like to die till I see and embrace the victory of the Nile.

"How shall I describe to you the transports of [the Queen] Maria Carolina? 'Tis not possible. She fainted, cried, kissed her husband, her children, walked frantic with pleasure about the room, cried, kissed and embraced every person near her, exclaiming: 'Oh, brave Nelson! Nelson, what do we not owe to you! Oh, victor, savior of Italy!'

"The Neapolitans are mad, and if you were here now you would be killed with kindness. Sonnets on sonnets, illuminations, rejoicing. Not a French dog dare show his face. How I glory in the honor of my country and my countryman! I walk and tread in air with pride, feeling I was born on the same land with the victor Nelson and his gallant band."

Nelson was the hero of the Nile, conqueror of the French Fleet, and destroyer of Napoleon's dreams for an eastern empire. However, he was about to lose the battle for his heart to Emma Hamilton. Like the legend of the Lorelei, Nelson the sailor would soon be sunk by the siren's song.

On the twenty-second of September, the *Vanguard* sailed into Naples Bay—very much unlike a glorious victor. A week before, she encountered a storm which took down her foremast, main topmast, and jibboom. To add to her inglorious appearance, she entered the bay under tow of a frigate.

From her curving balcony at Palazzo Sessa, Lady Hamilton enjoyed a sweeping view of the bay—Vesuvius and Sorrento to her left, the Island of Capri in the middle of the bay, and the hills of Posillipo to her right. For days she had been watching from her balcony, lined with pots of colorful geraniums, palms, and ferns, to catch sight of Nelson's ships.

Sir William Hamilton, the British Ambassador, had written to Nelson promising that "a pleasant apartment is ready for you in my house, and Emma is looking for the softest pillows, to repose the few wearied limbs you have left."

The usual cry of the street vendors, the tinkling sound of mandolins accompanying quavering tenor voices, and the braying of donkeys—all this changed when the *Vanguard* came into view. The air was filled with "Rule Britannia," and "See the Conquering Hero Comes."

A fleet of hundreds of odd-sized boats took off from the shore as soon as the *Vanguard* came within sight. King Ferdinand ordered his state barge rowed miles out to greet his "deliverer and preserver." One of the boats, loaded with musicians, loudly played "Rule Britannia." Neapolitans waved and shouted from the other boats bobbing around in the deep blue water.

Not to be outdone by the King, Lady Hamilton arranged to have Sir William's barge rowed alongside the *Vanguard.* She was the first to come bounding aboard.

Nelson stood there with his cocked hat partly covering the wound on his forehead, the empty sleeve of his gold-braided coat pinned back, and his one good eye taking in the amazing scene. Not the least amazing was Lady Hamilton's outfit! She wore a long white dress, the buttons embroidered with an "N" for Nelson. Her sash sported the red, white, and blue colors of the British flag. Her blue shawl was adorned with gold anchors, and miniature anchors dangled from her ears!

"Alongside came my honored friends," Nelson wrote to his wife Fanny. "The scene in the boat was terribly affecting—up flew her ladyship, exclaiming: 'O God, is it possible?' She fell into my arm more dead than alive. Tears, however, soon set matters to rights. I hope some day to have the pleasure of introducing you to Lady Hamilton; she is one of the best women in this world."

Lady Hamilton was then a beautiful woman, thirty-three years old. Her husband, Sir William, was sixty-eight. Emma had been born of extremely poor parents in Cheshire, England. With her pretty face and inexperience, she set out for London to find her own way in life.

At seventeen, she was destitute and wrote pitiful,

pleading letters to her friend, Charles Greville, to give her a home. In four years with him, she learned the basic refinements of society and good manners.

"Consider what a charming creature she would have been," wrote Greville, "if she had been blessed with the advantages of an early education, and had not been spoilt by the indulgence of every caprice."

In 1784, Sir William Hamilton visited his nephew, Greville, and met Emma for the first time. He found her charming, and agreed to have her "shipped to Italy." Arriving at Naples in the spring of 1786, Emma adapted well to her new life.

Sir William and Emma traveled to England and were married in September of 1791. They returned to the Ambassador's house at Palazzo Sessa, and Emma Hart was now Lady Hamilton. She soon gained prominence in the Court of Naples. By the time Nelson arrived in the *Vanguard*, Emma was a close friend of Queen Maria Carolina.

Nelson had business to complete at Naples—the most important was the repair of his crippled ships. He had many official business letters to write, and therefore decided to stay in a hotel while the *Vanguard* was under repair. Lady Hamilton would not hear of such nonsense, and insisted that he live in the ambassador's house. Palazzo Sessa soon became the headquarters for Nelson's social activities.

In a short time, those in Naples heard of the reaction in England to the victory of the Nile.

Upon hearing the news, Lord Spencer had been so excited that he fell unconscious to the floor!

"His joy had mastered him," exclaimed Lady Spencer.

"Joy, joy, joy to you," she wrote to Nelson in a letter bubbling over with rapture, "brave, gallant, immortalized Nelson! May that great God, whose cause you so valiantly support, protect and bless you to the end of your brilliant career! Such a race surely never was run.

"My heart is absolutely bursting with different sensations of joy, of gratitude, of pride, of every emotion, on hearing of her Country's glory—and all produced by you, my dear, my good friend."

King George III was at Weymouth when the news reached him, and, for the first time in his life he was struck speechless!

Spontaneous demonstrations swept over all England—church bells ringing, guns firing, bonfires blazing, and men marching. The crowds celebrating in the streets of London burst out singing "God Save the King," and "Rule Britannia."

Admiral Nelson was given the title "Baron Nelson of the Nile." With the title he received a yearly sum of 2,000 pounds. His Majesty ordered gold medals struck for Nelson and all his Captains. The city of London presented them with swords. All the officers received silver medals, and the enlisted men were awarded medals of copper.

Nelson had never been so financially well-off in his life. The East India Company showed its gratitude with a handsome 10,000 pounds. The Emperor of Russia sent a gold box set with diamonds. The Sultan of Turkey presented a diamond aigrette of great value. The Sultan's mother sent a beautiful box set with diamonds and other jewels. King Ferdinand of the Two Sicilies (Naples, Southern Italy, and Sicily) sent a beautifully decorated sword, and the King of Sardinia still another box ornamented with diamonds.

Congratulatory messages arrived from other countries of Europe, but few were received with as much gratitude as the one from Lord St. Vincent.

"God be praised, and you and your gallant band rewarded by a grateful country for the greatest achievement the history of the world can produce. Remember me kindly to Troubridge and all your heroes."

The strangest gift of all was from one of Nelson's own captains. Hallowell in the *Swiftsure* had hooked up a section of the mainmast from *L'Orient* and had it hauled aboard. He then ordered his carpenters to fashion a coffin for Nelson from the wood and spikes in the mast! He wrote;

"My Lord:

Herewith I send you a coffin made of part of *L'Orient*'s mainmast, that when you are tired of life, you may be buried in one of your own trophies—but may that period be distant is the sincere wish of your obedient and much obliged servant.

Ben Hallowell."

However great the acclaim in England, Nelson himself did not hear it first hand. What he did hear was the extravagant praise in Naples—led by Lady Hamilton. Flattery and admiration were generously lavished on him, and soon his heart was lost to Emma.

"Naples is a dangerous place, and we must keep clear of it," Nelson wrote to Lord St. Vincent. "I am writing opposite Lady Hamilton, therefore you will not be surprised at the glorious jumble of this letter. Were your Lordship in my place, I much doubt if you could write so well—our hearts and our hands must be all in a flutter."

Nelson had resolved to be "not more than four or five days at Naples, for these times are not for idleness." But this resolve was soon forgotten under the spell of Naples, Emma, the luxury of living at the elegant Palazzo Sessa, and the extravagance of the Court. Without realizing it, Nelson was falling completely in love with Emma Hamilton.

"Her manners are perfectly unpolished," Sir Gilbert Elliot wrote, "of course very easy, though not with the ease of good breeding—excessively good humored, and wishing to please and be admired by all ages and sorts of persons. One wonders at the application and pains she has taken to make herself what she is. With men her language and conversation are exaggerations of anything I ever heard anywhere."

Nelson, however, through the eyes of one hopelessly in love, saw a completely different creature.

"In every point of view, from ambassadress to the duties of domestic life, I never saw your equal. That elegance of manners, accomplishments, and, above all, your goodness of heart, is unparalleled", he wrote.

King Ferdinand and Queen Maria Carolina presided over a small country where great wealth and extravagance in the Court contrasted sharply with the poverty all around them. The Queen was the sister of Marie Antoinette, Queen of France, whose gaiety and flippancy earned a lasting, though inglorious, niche in the history of France and the French Revolution.

Fun-loving Ferdinand enjoyed playing both the role of His Majesty and Court fool. His buffoonery set the tone for a playful Court bent on thoroughgoing pleasure. The King enjoyed shooting birds for sport, although killing great numbers of defenseless birds was hardly sporting. At times he amused himself by dressing like a street vendor or fisherman and mingling among his people. It was only when his survival was threatened that the King showed any spark of dignity or practical thought.

The Kingdom of Naples—like a fool's paradise—was surrounded by a world crumbling under a wave of revolution and horror. With the irresponsible King and his nervous, headstrong Queen, the government was in the worst state imaginable. In fact, it was no secret that Lord Acton, the Prime Minister, and the Queen ruled the country. Lady Hamilton was the close confidante of the Queen, and delighted in the conniving and intrigue of the Court.

The doting Sir William approved of Emma's confidences with the Queen, though much went on without his knowledge. Hamilton's principal interest was in archeology and collecting ancient objects of art. Browsing for thirty-five years among the ruins of Vesuvius at Pompeii had provided him with his main diversion, and also a fine collection of antiques.

Nelson, the great seagoing Admiral of the Nile, was now in "strange waters." Under the double charms of Emma and the Queen, he became the champion of their causes—their knight in shining armor.

"Lady Hamilton is an angel," Nelson wrote. "She has honored me by being my ambassadress to the Queen—therefore she has my implicit confidence and is worthy of it."

Emma's intentions may have been good, but she

influenced Nelson in favoring the Queen's plots and plans. The Queen was motivated by hatred and revenge against the French for the beheading of her sister, Marie Antoinette, and by fear of the revolutionary Jacobins in her own country.

The French had overthrown the Papal Government a year before, and were occupying the Roman Republic. The nearness of the enemy was considered a threat to Naples. Nelson agreed with the Queen and Lady Hamilton that the French should be attacked and driven out.

In mid-October, Nelson sailed in the *Vanguard* with four other ships to give support to Captain Ball at Malta. He found the French commandant, Vaubois, holding out at Valetta with no means of obtaining food or other supplies. The fight was going well with good cooperation between the Maltese, Neapolitan, and British troops. Nelson personally accepted the surrender of the nearby Island of Gozo, and returned to Naples to resume plans for attacking Rome.

Under the command of the Austrian General Mack, King Ferdinand had 30,000 troops ready to advance on Rome. Nelson first met the General in November, at the beautiful country palace at Caserta. The spacious gardens, sparkling cascades, and magnificent palace were an opulent oasis, in the midst of the poverty-stricken countryside. Sir William and Lady Hamilton served as interpreters, since the General and the Admiral spoke no Italian.

It was planned that Mack would advance with his columns into Rome. At the same time, Nelson would sail up the coast with four thousand troops and six hundred cavalry to seize Leghorn. The army was paraded for Nelson, and described by the General as "the finest army in Europe."

The two-way prong, by land and by sea, met with brief success. The sea-borne part of the campaign landed at Leghorn, and the French ships in port were seized. Troubridge was left in charge. He was also given the task of breaking up the supply line of the French along the coast at Genoa and the Riviera. Nelson then returned to Naples.

General Mack led his troops into Rome, dusty and fatigued, though making a great show in numbers. The French General in command of the garrison decided he could not make a stand at Rome, and withdrew to better defensive ground at Civita Castellana. Five hundred French troops were left behind at Castle St. Angelo, along the Tiber River.

In triumph King Ferdinand entered Rome with his troops on the twenty-ninth of November. A showy entry it was! Bands played and banners waved as the motley thousands poured into Rome. However, they soon proved better at parading than fighting.

The French counterattacked with only 3,000 men against a mass of 19,000 scattered and poorly organized Neapolitan troops. The Neapolitans did not stay to fight. They retreated so fast that it turned into a footrace—led back to Naples by the King himself!

General Mack had displayed poor leadership over the 30,000 disorganized troops hailed as "the finest in Europe." The Neapolitan officers were no better. Their primary concern was to avoid getting hurt!

"The officers did not lose much honor," said Nelson in contempt, "for God knows they had not much to lose. But they lost all they had."

Reaching Naples safely was one matter—staying there was quite another. The attack on Rome had stirred up a hornet's nest against the Court at Naples. The King had shown the courage of a rabbit and the Queen was in a state of panic! The Court's only thought was to flee to Palermo, Sicily, quickly and quietly so the populace would not know about it.

Great secrecy was required in transporting the entire royal family and their priceless possessions to Palermo. Sir William and Emma packed their valuables at Palazzo Sessa. Crates, boxes, and bags were hastily crammed with everything from Emma's 500 pounds' worth of diamonds to Sir William's prized vases and antiques.

A great many packages and crates arrived at the Embassy from the Royal Palace, Palazzo Reale, delivered by sailors and marines from Nelson's ships. They were marked "Stores for Nelson." Furs, tapestries, jewelry, bronze and ivory figures, paintings, gold and money were securely sealed in the boxes. The secret cargo loaded on board the *Vanguard* was valued at 2,500,000 pounds.

It was a cold, blustery night when the royal family made their escape from Palazzo Reale on December 21. A secret underground passage led from the palace to the breakwater where British boats waited for them.

That evening Nelson and the Hamiltons, after dining at the Embassy, attended a reception given by the Turkish ambassador. Here, Nelson received a sable cape and a jeweled, plume-like ornament called a "chelengk" from one of the Turkish Imperial turbans.

They excused themselves early from the reception,

and made their way on foot to the palace. Emma found the Queen in hysterics, and the Royal children crying. She proved herself a pillar of strength by helping them through the dark, damp passageway. Nelson had gone to see that the boats and barges were brought to the tunnel exit, near the boat landing. A lantern swung from his hand as he stumbled along the dark, subterranean tunnel to meet them.

Nelson led the shivering children and the frightened women to the exit, where they were greeted by a howling wind. The waves crashed against the rocks with booming force and flying spray, warning them of what lay ahead.

With reassuring words, Nelson and his men helped the ladies and children into the boats and then rowed off into the night. Before ten o'clock, the seasick passengers were helped on board the *Vanguard,* as the stormy wind whipped the waves against the ship's side.

"Merry Christmas" or "Buon Natale" had a hollow ring as the *Vanguard* plunged through the stormy seas.

"It blew harder than I have ever experienced since I have been at sea," Nelson wrote.

The ship's topsails were shattered, the King's priest broke his arm, and the Duchess of Castelcicala had a nasty gash on her head. Six-year-old Prince Alberto died of convulsions in Lady Hamilton's arms.

Emma's calm courage during the entire rough voyage was admired by all the officers on board. Leading everyone in the "admiration department" was Nelson himself:

"Our dear Lady Hamilton, whom to see is to admire, but to know, are to be added honor and respect. Her head and heart surpass her beauty, which cannot be equalled by anything I have seen."

Old Sir William, helpful and kind as he was during the passage, was not much of a seaman. During the height of the booming gale Emma was astonished to find him with a loaded pistol in each hand.

"He was resolved," she wrote, "not to die with the 'guggle-guggle-guggle' of salt water in his throat—and therefore he was prepared, as soon as he felt the ship sinking, to shoot himself!"

Christmas Day had come and gone with little celebration. All were grateful that the stormy voyage had come to an end.

CHAPTER THIRTEEN

"WHEREVER THERE IS WATER TO FLOAT A SHIP WE ARE SURE TO FIND YOU IN THE WAY"

The flag of his Sicilian Majesty flew from the mainmast of the *Vanguard,* as Lord Nelson and his royal passengers approached Palermo. The ship anchored on the day after Christmas. The King and Queen, the royal retinue, the Hamiltons, Neapolitan nobles, British merchants, and servants were all rowed ashore. Lord Nelson and Captain Hardy had given up their quarters on the crowded ship, and Hardy was glad to resume a normal shipboard routine.

Admiral Nelson went ashore to live with the Hamiltons in a palatial villa. He paid for most of the cost of maintaining the luxurious quarters and the sumptuous living. Wealth had long escaped Nelson, and his money from the victory at the Nile was dwindling away.

Not long after this, King Ferdinand and his Court

sailed out of Naples and on January 23, 1799, the French army marched in. They established the Parthenopean Republic by force, though without the support of most of the Neapolitans. The feeble resistance of the peasantry was not enough to slow down the triumphal entry.

Nelson now received bad news from Malta as well as from Naples. The Maltese were living in misery, for the French troops at Valetta continued to hold out. Supply ships that had been sent to feed the starving people of Malta were being captured by the thieving ships of the Barbary States. Captain Ball was placed in charge of recapturing Malta from the French.

"I am delighted at our going back to the relief of the poor Maltese," Ball wrote. "You have no conception of their suffering at our leaving them." The French troops, who were holding out without a supply line, "have nearly eaten all the dogs, cats, horses and mules in the garrisons."

At the end of March, Captain Troubridge, in the *Culloden,* was sent to Naples to blockade the port and offer support to the loyalist forces. Nelson placed under his command the *Minotaur, Zealous, Swiftsure, Seahorse,* the bomb ship *Perseus,* and the sloop *El Corso.*

Troubridge's orders were to: "Blockade the city and towns in the Bay of Naples—to prevent the French forces from getting any supplies of corn or other articles by sea. The Island of Procida, affording the anchorage desired, use your endeavours to seize and get possession of Procida, if possible—and reinstate the Governor in command. Use every means to conciliate the affections of the loyal inhabitants, and also those of the Islands of Ischia and Capri.

"Communicate with the loyal inhabitants of Naples and all the Northern coast of the Kingdom of Naples, to induce them to return their allegiance to his Sicilian Majesty, and to take arms to liberate their country from French tyranny."

Captain Troubridge found an active group of loyalists at Naples who gladly welcomed him. They were anxious for the return of their King. Their leader was Cardinal Fabrizio Ruffo. His large band of followers consisted of a hodge-podge of peasants, escaped criminals, priests and friars, rabble from the streets of Naples, and many of the soldiers who had taken part in the hasty retreat from Rome.

The French troops found the streets of Naples unsafe—Ruffo's ragged army seemed to be everywhere. The revolutionary republicans were beaten by Ruffo's loyalists. Many of them were killed, others thrown into prison, and the streets were littered with corpses.

Soon the French occupation forces were forced to retreat into the country, and then into the strongly fortified Castel St. Elmo high on a ridge above Naples. The enormous castle offered a commanding view of the Bay as well as a strong defensive position. The Neapolitan Jacobins who cooperated with the French republicans holed up in the two stone fortifications, Castel dell' Uovo and Castel Nuovo, along the waterfront.

Good news seemed to be mixed with bad. The improving situation at Naples, through the efforts of Troubridge and Ruffo, was soon followed with the news that a French Fleet was entering the Mediterranean. Twenty-five ships-of-the-line were reported at Toulon. From there, they might sail either for Malta to reinforce the French force, or to Alexandria to support Napoleon's land-bound army.

In the meantime, a fine new British flagship, HMS *Foudroyant* of eighty guns, arrived at Palermo. Nelson, now Rear Admiral of the Red, shifted his colorful flag from the *Vanguard* on the eighth of June. He also transferred Captain Hardy, some of his officers, midshipmen, and petty officers to the *Foudroyant*.

Nelson's splendid new ship hardly offset the bad news that Lord St. Vincent was leaving the Mediterranean command. St. Vincent's health was so poor that he could not carry the heavy work load any longer.

"We have a report that you are going home," Nelson wrote to him. "This distresses us most exceedingly, and myself in particular. For the sake of our Country, do not quit us at this serious moment. If, my dear Lord, I have any weight in your friendship, let me entreat you to rouse the sleeping lion."

The letter was written in vain. Lord St. Vincent received it after he had already turned over the Mediterranean command to Lord Keith. That marked the end of a happy command relationship in the Mediterranean.

Nelson was now a busier man than ever, with a great deal of responsibility.

"My public correspondence," he wrote to his brother William, "besides the business of sixteen sail-of-the-line, and all our commerce, is with Petersburg, Constantinople [Istanbul], the Consul at

Smyrna, Egypt, the Turkish and Russian Admirals, Triest, Vienna, Tuscany, Minorca, Earl St. Vincent and Lord Spencer. This over, what time can I have for private correspondence?"

One of his biggest problems was the persistent fears and demands of the King and Queen of the Two Sicilies. Convinced by them that he should go to Naples, Nelson sailed from Palermo with the Hamiltons in the *Foudroyant*. He arrived with his squadron late in the evening of June 24. As the *Foudroyant* sailed into Naples Bay alone, Nelson could see the white flags of truce flying from the two castles Uovo and Nuovo, where many of the Jacobins had fled. He soon learned that a 21-day armistice with the Jacobins had been signed. This would allow them time to evacuate the castles and leave for France.

When the rest of Nelson's ships sailed into the Bay on the morning of June 25, the Jacobins were delighted. They thought French ships were arriving to give them passage. They soon learned, however, that the ships were British, and that Nelson, acting on the request of the King and Queen at Palermo, would settle for nothing but unconditional surrender.

Hearing that Nelson had cancelled the terms of his negotiations, Cardinal Ruffo, greatly upset, arrived on board the *Foudroyant*. The Hamiltons did their best to translate the quick staccato of his Italian which poured out like machine-gun bullets. Nelson had just come from the Royal Court, and considered his surrender terms as the only ones officially in effect.

Ruffo had to return and inform the enemy Jacobins that they could not have the terms he had agreed upon. Nelson did not consider them an "enemy" because they were acting against their own king—he therefore treated them as "rebels and traitors."

On June 29 an interesting prisoner was brought aboard the *Foudroyant*—Commodore Francesco Caracciolo, the head of the rebellious republican Navy. He had accompanied the royal family to Palermo and, with their permission, he returned to Naples. Here he immediately joined the republican forces and fought against the British and Royal Neapolitan navies.

Caracciolo had fired on the Neapolitan frigate *La Minerva,* killing two men and wounding four others. When the republican cause crumbled, he fled to his mother's villa near Naples. However, before he could escape from the country, he was betrayed by a servant loyal to the King, and thrown into prison. Brought aboard the *Foudroyant* from prison, his clothes were in rags, he was dirty, unshaven, and heavily chained.

Nelson asked that a Board of Naval Officers of His Sicilian Majesty be assembled to try him. The Board found the charge of rebellion fully proved against him, and sentenced Caracciolo to suffer death "by hanging him at the fore yard-arm of *La Minerva,* at five o'clock this evening—to cause him to hang there until sunset, when you will have his body cut down, and thrown into the sea."

Had he lived, Francesco Caracciolo would have been a rebel who failed a lost cause. Upon his death he became a martyred hero. Today, the main street curving along the Naples waterfront, between the park and the Bay, is named Via Caracciolo. Still standing, Castel dell' Uovo juts out into the Bay of Naples, Castel Nuovo is a prominent landmark from the port, and Castel St. Elmo rises high on the hill beyond. If stones could talk, what stories these old castles might tell!

Troubridge eventually succeeded in forcing St. Elmo to surrender with the help of Russian and Royalist troops. This accomplished, the city of Naples was again safe for the return of the King and Queen.

Due to a possible French attack on Minorca, Lord Keith wrote to Nelson in July asking for ships. Nelson, however, did not send them. He was busy fighting the French in the Kingdom of Naples and many of his sailors and marines were then fighting ashore. Nelson was well aware that disobedience in the Navy of his day was an extremely serious matter.

"I am fully aware of the act I have committed, but sensible of my loyal intentions," he wrote to the First Lord of the Admiralty. "I am prepared for any fate which may await my disobedience. Capua and Gaeta [near Naples] will soon fall. The moment the French scoundrels are out of this Kingdom, I shall send eight or nine ships-of-the-line to Minorca." His decision not to send the ships at once brought a sharp letter from the Admiralty.

The King had joined Nelson on the *Foudroyant* during July. He held court on board and entertained as though he were in his own castle. On the first anniversary of the Battle of the Nile, a big celebration, with music and a burst of fireworks, was given by the King.

"The King dined with me," Nelson wrote to Fanny, "and when His Majesty drank my health, a Royal salute of twenty-one guns was fired from all his Sicilian Majesty's ships of war, and from all the castles. In the evening there was a general illumination. A large vessel was fitted out like a Roman galley—on its oars were fixed lamps, and in the center was erected a rostral column with my name.

"More than 2,000 variegated lamps were suspended round the Vessel. An orchestra was fitted up, and filled with the very best musicians and singers. In short, my dear Fanny, the beauty of the whole is beyond my powers of description."

Without once going ashore, the King left with Nelson for Palermo. The *Foudroyant* sailed out of Naples Bay on the fifth of August, and arrived at Palermo on the eighth. There, the King honored Nelson with the title of Duke of Brontë, and he received a beautiful diamond-hilted sword. The estate that went with the title was in the shadow of the active volcano, Mount Etna. The name Brontë was most appropriate—in Italian it means "thunder!"

King George III gave Nelson permission to use the title, and from then on he signed his name "Nelson and Brontë." By now Nelson had so many ribbons and stars that he cut a colorful and conspicuous figure in any crowd. One of his former associates, upon seeing him at the Neapolitan Court, wrote: "He is covered with stars, ribbons and medals, more like a Prince of an Opera, than the Conqueror of the Nile."

The gay life at Palermo picked up again in spite of Nelson's busy work load. Keith had sailed into the Atlantic in pursuit of the French Fleet, and Nelson temporarily bore the entire burden of command in the Mediterranean. One of his continuing tasks was keeping the Maltese supplied with enough food to prevent them from starving. Even the stalwart Troubridge was moved at the pitiful conditions on Malta.

"I am not very tender-hearted," he wrote to Nelson, "but the distress here would move even a Neapolitan."

Unknown to Nelson, Napoleon managed to escape from Egypt in October. He sailed in a Venetian frigate, and successfully evaded the British blockading force under Sir Sydney Smith. To have the arch-enemy slip away and return to Toulon was a crushing blow.

"No crusader ever returned with more humility," Nelson wrote to Sir Sydney. However, the "crusader" could now rise again to plague Europe.

"If it had not been for you English," Napoleon fretted, "I should have been Emperor of the East. But wherever there is water to float a ship we are sure to find you in the way."

The lavish living at the Court at Palermo was the subject of much scandalous talk. Nelson's close contact with the corrupt Court caused much gossip. This hurt his fellow officers profoundly. Captain Ball at Malta wrote that he was "quite concerned at the many severe paragraphs which have been put in the newspapers."

Lady Minto, the wife of the former Viceroy at Corsica, had a very poor impression of the life at Palermo.

"Nelson and the Hamiltons all lived together in a house of which he bore the expense, which was enormous, and every sort of gaming went on half the night. Nelson used to sit with large parcels of gold before him, and generally go to sleep—Lady Hamilton taking from the heap without counting, and playing with his money to the amount of 500 pounds a night. Her rage is play, and Sir William says when he is dead she will be a beggar. She sits at the Councils, and rules everything and everybody."

Captain Troubridge was deeply disturbed by these reports.

"Pardon me, my Lord," he wrote to Nelson. "It is my sincere esteem for you that makes me mention it. I know you can have no pleasure in sitting up all night at cards. Why then sacrifice your health, comfort, purse, ease, everything—to the customs of a country, where your stay cannot be long?

"Your Lordship is a stranger to half that happens, or the talk it occasions. If you knew what your friends feel for you, I am sure you would cut all the nocturnal parties. The gambling of the people at Palermo is publicly talked of everywhere. I beseech your Lordship to leave off."

Because of his love for Lady Hamilton, Nelson could not see how steadily she was ruining his reputation, and overlooked her constant interference with the affairs of state and the British Navy.

Troubridge was bold enough to write directly to Nelson about it. He did not hesitate to mention a recent instance of Lady Hamilton's "known interference" involving a marine sentenced to death for mutiny.

Captain Hardy of the *Foudroyant* minded his own business, and kept aloof from any involvement in the affair. However, when Lady Hamilton became involved in his business, he dealt with the situation in his own effective way.

One of the boat crews from the *Foudroyant* had

misbehaved, and the men asked Lady Hamilton to use her influence that they might escape punishment. She spoke to Captain Hardy about it. He nodded in complete understanding, and apparent sympathy for what she was trying to do.

When the punishment for their misdemeanor was given, it was doubled. Instead of a dozen lashes, they each received two dozen! Hardy notified her that this would be the standard practice in the future, whenever she interfered with the orderly punishment of transgressors. That was the last time any of the men asked Lady Hamilton for protection!

Hardy returned to England in December, and Captain Berry relieved him as commanding officer of the *Foudroyant*. Rear Admiral Nelson, after almost six months as acting Commander-in-chief in the Mediterranean, was also about to be relieved of this responsibility.

Vice Admiral Keith returned to the Mediterranean in January, 1800, and ordered Nelson to meet him at Leghorn. On the twentieth of January, Nelson was piped on board Keith's flagship, HMS *Queen Charlotte*. The meeting was a frosty one.

While in England, Keith had heard many rumors, and was determined to put a stop to the Palermo nonsense. Eager to get a first-hand look at the situation, Keith sailed with Nelson on the twenty-fifth for a visit to Palermo.

"The whole," he wrote, "was a scene of fulsome vanity and absurdity all the long eight days I was at Palermo."

Nelson and Keith then sailed to blockade Malta, arriving there in mid-February. Soon after they arrived, a French squadron was reported approaching Malta. It was a misty day when Nelson sailed off, with three ships-of-the-line, to chase the French.

On the morning of the eighteenth, the sound of distant guns led the *Foudroyant* to the *Alexander*. She was chasing and firing at four French ships. A young midshipman by the name of Parsons wrote an excellent description of the battle that followed.

" 'Deck there!' a lieutenant from aloft in the *Foudroyant* called out. 'The stranger is evidently a man-of-war. She is a line-of-battle ship, my Lord, and going large on the starboard tack.'

" 'Ah! an enemy, Mr. Stains! I pray God it may be *Le Genereux*! The signal for a general chase, Sir Ed'ard [Captain Berry]. Make the *Foudroyant* fly!'

"Thus spake the heroic Nelson. Every exertion that emulation could inspire was used to crowd the squadron with canvas—the *Northumberland* taking the lead, with the flagship close on her quarter.

" 'This will not do, Sir Ed'ard—it is certainly *Le Genereux*, and to my flagship she can alone surrender. Sir Ed'ard, we must and shall beat the *Northumberland*!'

" 'I will do my utmost, my Lord,' Captain Berry responded. He quickly shouted orders: 'Get the engine to work on the sails [a hand pump to wet the sails and hold the wind for more speed]. Hang butts of water to the stays. Pipe the hammocks down, and each man place shot in them. Slack the stays, knock up the wedges, and give the masts play. Start off the water, Mr. James, and pump the ship.'

"The *Foudroyant* gained, and finally took the lead. Nelson, noticing that the quartermaster at the helm was not paying close attention to what he was doing, admonished: 'I'll knock you off your perch, you rascal, if you are so inattentive! Sir Ed'ard, send your best quartermaster to the weather wheel.'

" 'A strange sail ahead of the chase,' called the lookout.

" 'Youngster, to the masthead! What—going without your glass? Be d—— to you! Let me know what she is immediately.'

" 'A sloop of war or frigate, my Lord,' the young midshipman shouted down.

" 'Demand her number.'

" 'The *Success,* my Lord.'

" 'Signal her to cut off the flying enemy. Great odds though—thirty-two small guns to eighty large ones!'

" 'The *Success,* my Lord, has hove-to athwart-hawse of *Le Genereux,* and is firing her larboard broadside. The Frenchman has hoisted his tri-colour, with a rear-admiral's flag.'

" 'Bravo—*Success!* At her again!'

" 'She has wore round, my Lord, and is firing her starboard broadside. It has winged her, my Lord. Her flying kites are flying away altogether.'

"The enemy was close on the *Success,* who was about to receive *Le Genereux*'s tremendous broadside," continued Parsons. "*Le Genereux* opened fire on the little frigate, and every person stood aghast, afraid of the consequences. The smoke cleared away, and there was the *Success*—crippled, it is true, but, bulldog-like, bearing up after the enemy.

" 'Signal the *Success* to discontinue the action and come under my stern,' Lord Nelson said to Berry. 'She has done well, for her size! Try a shot from the lower deck at her, Sir Ed'ard.'

"'It goes over her,' said Berry of the first shot fired at *Le Genereux.*

"'Beat to quarters, and fire coolly and deliberately at her masts and yards.'"

Parsons' story continued: "*Le Genereux* at this moment opened fire on us. As a shot passed through the mizzen stay-sail, Lord Nelson, patting one of the youngsters on the head, asked him jocularly how he relished the music? Observing something like alarm depicted on his countenance, he consoled him with the information that Charles XII ran away from the first shot he heard, though afterwards he was called 'The Great,'—and deservedly, from his bravery. 'I, therefore,' said Nelson, 'hope much from you in the future.'

"Here the *Northumberland* opened her fire, and down came the tri-coloured ensign, amidst the thunder of our united cannon."

After the battle, Sir Edward Berry boarded *Le Genereux.* He soon returned with Rear Admiral Perree's sword, and reported that the Admiral was dying, having lost both legs from the raking fire of the *Success.*

Nelson was elated! He had now taken twelve of the thirteen line-of-battle ships from the Nile. Only *Le Guillaume Tell* remained to be captured.

Lord Nelson reported his capture of *Le Genereux* to Admiral Keith on the following day, but Keith received the news without enthusiasm.

"Lord Keith received my account and myself like a philosopher," Nelson wrote to Sir William Hamilton. "It did not, that I could perceive, cause a pleasing muscle in his face."

Keith then left Nelson in charge of the blockade of

Malta, and asked him to use a better base for his operations than Palermo. Syracuse, Augusta, and Messina were all suggested. However, Nelson ignored his suggestion, and sailed for Palermo on the tenth of March. Berry was sent back with the *Foudroyant* to Malta.

Inside the harbor at La Valetta, *Le Guillaume Tell* waited for a chance to run the British blockade and return to France. She sailed out of the harbor on the night of March 29. Fortunately, the *Foudroyant* had arrived a few hours before!

"If the *Foudroyant* had not arrived," Troubridge wrote, "nothing we have could have looked at her."

Captain Henry Blackwood, in the frigate *Penelope,* first sighted *Le Guillaume Tell,* and followed on her heels like a terrier after a wolfhound. The big 80-gun French ship could have smashed the *Penelope* with one of her powerful broadsides, but she was intent on gaining distance to escape. While maneuvering to keep clear of her guns, the frigate succeeded in shooting down the main and mizzen topmasts of *Le Guillaume Tell.*

With the *Tell's* rigging damaged, the other British ships were able to catch up. The *Foudroyant* passed the *Penelope* and the 64-gun *Lion,* both of them having dropped back from the withering fire.

At six o'clock the next morning, the *Foudroyant* closed in with her eighty guns, matching the big French ship. In half an hour, her main and mizzenmast were shattered and crashed down. *Le Guillaume Tell* put up a stubborn fight, but Berry fought the *Foudroyant* well. Shortly after eight o'clock, the enemy's foremast was shot away and, without a mast left standing, *Le Guillaume Tell* struck her colors.

Thirteen out of thirteen French ships from the Nile were now accounted for! It was a clean sweep for the British.

"I am sensible of your kindness in wishing my presence at the finish of the Egyptian Fleet," Nelson wrote to Captain Berry, "but I have no cause for sorrow. The thing could not be better done, and I would not for all the world rob you of one particle of your well-earned laurels."

While Nelson was at Palermo with his flag flying from a transport, he received a letter from Lord Spencer.

"I should be very sorry that you did not accomplish that business in person, as *Le Guillaume Tell* is your due, and that ship ought not to strike to any other. If the enemy should come into the Mediterranean, I should be much concerned to hear that you learned of their arrival in that sea, either on shore or in a transport at Palermo."

Lord Minto (formerly Sir Gilbert Elliot) wrote in March from Vienna that he hoped Nelson would not go home until he had first taken Malta.

"He does not seem at all conscious of the sort of discredit he has fallen into, or the cause of it—for he still writes, not wisely, about Lady Hamilton and all that. But it is hard to condemn and use ill a hero for being foolish about a woman who has art enough to make fools of many wiser than an admiral."

The days were numbered for the Hamiltons as British representatives. Lord Elgin, who had visited Palermo on his way to Constantinople, had reported: "During a week's stay at Palermo, on my passage here, the necessity of a change in our representative appeared to me most urgent."

Sir William Hamilton's replacement as ambassador, Mr. Arthur Paget, would not permit Sir William to see his instructions upon arrival.

"I decided at once not to do so, for he would certainly have been obliged to show them to Lady Hamilton, who would have conveyed them next moment to the Queen. His Lordship's health is, I fear, sadly impaired, and I am assured that his fortune is fallen into the same state—in consequence of great losses which both his Lordship and Lady Hamilton have sustained at Faro and other games of hazard."

Nelson was also planning to leave the Mediterranean and return to England. He had not been well since the Battle of the Nile. His conduct at Naples and Palermo was not like that of the old Nelson. Some blamed his head wound, others blamed Lady Hamilton. It may have been a combination of both.

Queen Maria Carolina wanted to visit Vienna, and asked Nelson to take her along. He promptly took the *Foudroyant* and the *Alexander* away from their blockade duties at Malta, embarking the Queen, the Hamiltons, and their entourages. When Keith heard about this move, he wrote a letter absolutely forbidding him to use his ships-of-the-line! It arrived too late, however. Nelson had already sailed for Leghorn, arriving the middle of June.

Ten days after the *Foudroyant* sailed into the harbor at Leghorn, Admiral Keith arrived, and confronted Nelson personally. The Queen dissolved into tears, and panicked when he refused her passage in the *Foudroyant*.

"The Queen wept, concluding that royal tears were irresistible," Lady Minto wrote, "but he [Keith] remained unmoved, and would grant nothing but a frigate to convoy her own frigates to Trieste. He told her Lady Hamilton had had command of the fleet long enough!"

The entourage started across country from Leghorn to Ancona on the eleventh of July—the Queen, the Hamiltons, and Nelson. From Ancona, on the Adriatic Sea, the party embarked in a squadron of three Russian frigates and a brig, arriving at Trieste on the second of August. Thousands of people gathered, and shouts of "Viva Nelson" greeted the hero of the Nile.

At Vienna, Lady Minto described Nelson and Lady Hamilton.

"He has the same honest simple manners, and he is devoted to Emma. He thinks her quite an angel, and she leads him about like a keeper with a bear. He is a gig from ribands, orders and stars, but he is just the same with us as ever he was."

A sad farewell took place between Emma and the Queen at Vienna. Then Nelson and the Hamiltons continued on to Prague, Dresden, Magdeburg, and Hamburg, where grand receptions were held all along the way. Near Hamburg they took passage in a mail-packet for a storm-tossed crossing to Yarmouth, England. Upon their arrival on the sixth of November, enthusiastic crowds greeted Nelson. Three days later, he met Fanny and his father at Nerot's Hotel in London, after a separation of more than two and a half years.

Something new had been added to Lord Nelson's life during his absence—Lady Hamilton. The gossip about this great love affair had been well-circulated in London. Lady Nelson, however, was hardly prepared to meet the object of his affections clinging to his arm as they entered the hotel! It was not long before Fanny understandably confronted her husband with an ultimatum: "I am sick of hearing of dear Lady Hamilton, and am resolved that you shall give up either her or me."

It was inevitable that he and Fanny should separate respectfully, but permanently. Afterward, Nelson lived with the Hamiltons, leading a happy life, even though the society of London did not accept Emma. He provided well for Lady Nelson all of her life, and loved Lady Hamilton all of his life. Nelson did not become famous for his smooth domestic relations, but rather for his greatness as an admiral.

Nelson's "song of love" was a sad song. It was not a mere love affair that took the wind out of Nelson's sails—it was a till-death-do-us-part love.

CHAPTER FOURTEEN

"WE'LL SEND OUR BRAVE NELSON TO THRASH THEM AGAIN"

The cool, bracing English air worked miracles on Nelson's health, and in November he applied to the Admiralty for another assignment. He promptly got results!

On New Year's Day, 1801, Nelson was promoted to Vice Admiral of the Blue. His new flag snapped in the fresh breeze at Plymouth for the first time on the seventeenth of January, from the mast of the *San Josef*. This was a most appropriate flagship—he had captured the huge three-decker in the battle off Cape St. Vincent.

Assigned to the Channel Fleet, he would now serve under his old Commander-in-chief, Lord St. Vincent. Trouble with Denmark was threatening and Nelson was ordered to sail into the Baltic under a senior Vice Admiral, Sir Hyde Parker. As usual, Napoleon was the cause of the trouble.

Much of Britain's trade was with Denmark,

Sweden, and Russia—especially imports from those countries needed by the Royal Navy. These nations took offense when British ships stopped and searched their ships for contraband. Napoleon, having little to lose, freely offered these Baltic countries immunity from search by French ships.

Joining together, the Baltic States called their alliance the Armed Neutrality. This neutrality gave them great freedom in trading, and fat profits from the trade among the countries at war.

The "mad" Emperor of Russia, Czar Paul I, had been hostile to Great Britain for some time, and had placed an embargo on all British shipping. Denmark and Sweden, pushed by France, were on the verge of opposing British ships with force. The Danes resorted to sending their ships in large convoys, escorted by warships. After two armed clashes at sea with the British, Denmark agreed not to use armed convoys in her trade with France. The British ships could then properly search the ships and seize enemy goods in neutral ships.

France had slyly offered Malta to Russia when it was recaptured by the British in November of 1800. When Great Britain refused to turn the Island over to the Russian Emperor, he reacted with blind fury. The Czar promptly seized about 300 British merchant ships then in Russian ports. The crews were taken off, and marched inland as prisoners. British warehouses were locked, and trade with Russia was stopped.

Russia had been an uncertain ally of Great Britain after the Nile victory. However, the French had successfully turned the Czar against England by vain promises, and by sowing seeds of hatred against the British.

For service in the Baltic, Lord Nelson shifted his flag to a lighter ship, HMS *St. George,* on the twelfth of February, 1801. Later in the month, he dashed off to London to see his new daughter, Horatia, who had been born the end of January.

The *St. George* then set sail for Yarmouth, where Nelson joined Sir Hyde Parker, his new Commander-in-chief. Sir Hyde was then sixty-two, and had just married a girl of nineteen. His thoughts were primarily concerned with a farewell ball!

Eager to get on with the Baltic expedition, Nelson passed word to his friend Troubridge, who was now at the Admiralty. As a result, orders were issued to sail immediately, and Sir Hyde's party had to wait for the completion of more important business—the defeat or seizure of the ships of the Baltic States.

Sir Hyde was wealthy, cautious, and about to retire. His uppermost wish was to return from the Baltic expedition, alive and without loss of honor. Nelson's attitude toward the expedition differed sharply from Parker's.

On the tenth of March, Sir Hyde's flagship HMS *London* arrived at Yarmouth, but he was not too anxious to hurry on board. The cold, raw wind, ripping across the decks of the ships, did little to ease Nelson's impatience to get underway. Sir Hyde's flag finally fluttered from the mast of the *London,* and the ships weighed anchor on a chilly, blustery twelfth of March.

"It took us nearly an hour at daybreak to shovel down the snow from our tops and yards before we could weigh anchor," Lieutenant George Elliot in the *St. George* recorded.

The cold wind reddened ears, noses, and hands, as the men struggled with the frozen lines and canvas. Many of them had recently arrived from the Mediterranean, and they were not yet accustomed to winter weather. Few were dressed warmly enough for the Baltic.

Nelson had not had a chance to talk to Sir Hyde, who seemed to be trying to avoid a meeting with his spirited second-in-command. Although they were miles apart in temperament, Nelson felt Sir Hyde should at least ask him to his flagship for a conference to discuss plans.

"Our weather is very cold," Nelson wrote. "We have received much snow and sharp frost. I have not yet seen my Commander-in-chief, and have had no official communication whatever. All I have gathered of our first plans, I disapprove most exceedingly—honor may arise from them, good cannot.

"I hear we are likely to anchor outside Cronenburg Castle, instead of Copenhagen, which would give weight to our negotiations. A Danish Minister would think twice before he would put his name to war with England, when the next moment he would probably see his Master's Fleet in flames, and his Capital in ruins—but, 'out of sight out of mind' is an old saying."

Nelson, pacing back and forth on deck, wondered how he could communicate with his Commander-in-chief. He overheard Lieutenant Layman mention that he had previously caught a fine turbot near the Dogger Bank, where the ship would be passing.

"Do you think we could catch a turbot?" Nelson asked.

Lines were put over the side, and a turbot was caught! In spite of a choppy sea, a boat was lowered, and Nelson had the fish delivered to Sir Hyde. The boat returned with the Admiral's compliments and appreciation. The "ice" was broken, and a conference on board the *London* soon followed.

Late in the afternoon of March twentieth, the fleet anchored in the Kattegat, and Mr. Nicholas Vansittart, a representative of the Foreign Office, went down to Copenhagen. He was instructed to give Denmark forty-eight hours to withdraw from the coalition of Baltic States, or consider herself a belligerent. The terms were rejected by the Danes, and Vansittart returned on the twenty-third with news that great defenses were being prepared at Copenhagen.

On the twenty-sixth, Nelson shifted his flag to the lighter 74-gun HMS *Elephant,* under his old friend, Captain Foley. On the thirtieth, with a favorable northwest wind, the ships started down the Kattegat toward Copenhagen. The Swedish guns threatened on one side, and the Danish on the other. Since the Swedes did not open fire, the ships sailed closer to the Swedish coast while the Danes blazed away at the ships from their shore batteries.

"More powder and shot, I believe, never were thrown away," wrote Nelson, "for not one shot struck a single ship of the British Fleet. Some of our ships fired, but the *Elephant* did not return a single shot. I hope to reserve them for a better occasion."

The ships anchored a few miles from Copenhagen. On the thirty-first, Nelson and Parker sailed ahead in the frigate *Amazon* with Captain Edward Riou, a superior sailer, to reconnoiter the Danish positions. The days of futile negotiations clearly had given the Danes plenty of time to strengthen their defenses around Copenhagen.

To make a direct approach to the city, they would have to battle the powerful Trekroner batteries, which were built on pilings guarding the harbor and King's Channel. Along the shore heavy gun emplacements were prepared, and a line of eighteen ships paralleled the shore in King's Channel. Some of these ships, though mere hulks, were powerful floating gun platforms.

Farther off shore was a shoal called the Middle Ground, with an Outer Channel around the other side of it. To avoid the strongest defenses at the Trekroner batteries, Nelson decided to approach from around the Middle Ground shoal, and come up on the weaker end of King's Channel. He had twelve ships-of-the-line, four frigates, four sloops, seven bomb-ships, two fire-ships, and twelve gun-brigs. Parker, with the rest of his fleet, would make a show of force from the opposite direction.

Lieutenant Colonel William Stewart, with some of his army troops, was on board the *Elephant*. The night before the attack, a meeting was held.

"On board the *Elephant* the night of the first of April was an important one," Colonel Stewart recorded. "As soon as the fleet was at anchor, the gallant Nelson sat down at the table with a large party of his comrades in arms. He was in the highest spirits, and drank to a leading wind, and to the success of the ensuing day.

"Captains Foley, Hardy, Fremantle, Riou, Inman, Admiral Graves, his Lordship's second-in-command, and a few others to whom he was particularly attached, were of this interesting party—from which every man separated with feelings of admiration for their great leader, and with anxious impatience to follow him to the approaching battle."

Nelson stayed up most of the night writing instructions for his captains, and watching the wind and weather. Early the next morning, the wind was fair, and the ships were ready to sail in. The wind the day before had taken the ships south, and changed just before the battle to take them north.

The pilots decided at the last minute not to guide them in. The Danes had taken up all the channel buoys, and the passage was extremely treacherous. The master of the *Bellona* volunteered to lead the ships, and the attack was underway.

The *Agamemnon*, of Mediterranean fame, got off to a bad start by running aground. The *Bellona* and the *Russell*, 74-gun ships, succeeded in rounding the Middle Ground, but grounded on the shoal in King's Channel. They could still use their guns, although at that range they had little effect. Nelson's dozen ships-of-the-line at the outset were cut down to nine.

Noticing that the ships ahead had grounded, Captain Foley had the *Elephant* veer past into deeper water. Nelson quickly rearranged his battle order and hailed the *Ganges* to take its place ahead of the *Elephant*.

The slow, silent approach of sailing ships going into battle set the men's nerves taut with keen anticipation. The huge white sails towering overhead drew closer and closer to the enemy, as the gun crews waited eagerly by their cannon.

On the deck, orders to the wheel were repeated like a religious chant. As the first ship glided within range of the enemy batteries, the sudden thunder of guns came as an almost welcome relief from the ominous silence.

Sailing past the long line of stationary ships in King's Channel was a bloody row to pass. The ships formed a close column a mile and a half long.

Nelson's ships sailed into their assigned positions. As they anchored, the *Defiance* (74 guns) was in the lead position, followed in order by the *Monarch* (74), *Ganges* (74), *Elephant* (74), *Glatton* (50), *Ardent* (64), *Edgar* (74), *Iris* (50), *Polyphemus* (64), and the frigate *Desiree* (36 guns).

When fully engaged, almost 1,500 cannon opened up on each other. Flame leaped out of the muzzles, and the rumble of erupting gunpowder drowned out the crash of the cannon-balls. Fighting against a stationary enemy, Nelson said, was "no maneuvering—it was just downright fighting."

A cannon-ball struck the mainmast of the *Elephant*, and scattered splinters around the deck near Nelson. He smiled, and turned to Stewart.

"It is warm work, and this day may be the last to any of us at a moment!" he remarked. "But mark you—I would not be elsewhere for thousands!"

Sir Hyde Parker was still approaching at a distance against head winds with the larger ships-of-the-line. The fury of the battle alarmed him, and the sight of three of Nelson's ships aground told him at a glance that all was not going according to their plan.

He immediately called his officers around to discuss whether he should hoist the signal to discontinue the action.

One of his captains opposed the idea, and suggested that he first board the *Elephant* and consult Nelson. The captain shoved off from the *London.* At one o'clock, before his boat had arrived alongside the *Elephant,* Parker hoisted signal "39"—to cease action!

The signal lieutenant aboard the *Elephant* promptly reported the flag hoist to Nelson. But Nelson appeared not to have heard the report, so the Lieutenant repeated it, and asked what should be done. If Nelson also hoisted "39," according to regulations, it would mean the end of the battle. All his ships would then cease firing and withdraw.

Nelson told his Lieutenant to acknowledge that he had seen it—but not to repeat it. The Lieutenant turned to execute his orders.

"Is number '16'—for *close action*—still hoisted?" Nelson called.

The Lieutenant assured him that it was.

"Mind you keep it so!"

Stewart described Nelson's action on the deck: "He now walked the deck considerably agitated, which was always known by his moving the stump of his right arm. After a turn or two he said to me in a quick manner: 'Do you know what's shown on board the Commander-in-chief? Number 39!' On asking him what that meant, he answered: 'Why, to leave off action. Leave off action!' he repeated, and then added, with a shrug: 'Now damn me if I do!'

"He also observed to Captain Foley: 'You know

Foley, I have only one eye—I have a right to be blind sometimes!' Then, with an archness peculiar to his character, putting the glass to his blind eye, he exclaimed: 'I really do not see the signal!' "

From his flagship *Defiance*, Rear Admiral Graves saw Sir Hyde's signal, and repeated it. However, following Nelson's example, he still kept his "close action" flags flying and continued to fire.

Captain Riou's division of small ships was then fighting heroically near the powerful Trekroner batteries—three frigates, the *Amazon* (38 guns), *Blanche* (36), and *Alemer* (32 guns); two sloops and two fire-ships. They were withstanding a withering return fire, and when the signal to "leave off action" was hoisted in the *London*, they were within easy sight of the flagship. Reluctantly, Riou broke off firing, and turned his ship, the *Amazon*, away from the action.

"What will Nelson think of us?" he remarked.

A hail of shot ripped into the ship. His clerk and several marines were killed in short order.

"Come then, my boys, let us all die together!"

Riou had spoken his last words to his men—a shot almost immediately cut him in two. Nelson had lost one of his bravest and finest captains.

The losses on both sides were heavy because of the great concentration of guns in a small battle area and little mobility for the ships. On board the burning Danish flagship *Dannesborg*, 270 were killed and wounded. Commodore Fischer had shifted his flag to the *Holstein*. The *Holstein* and the *Infrodstrettin* were both smashed and shattered, their flags shot away. Commodore Fischer again shifted his flag to the Trekroner batteries.

Some of the Danish ships' guns blazed away after they had apparently surrendered. By two o'clock, most of the Danish line could not return fire. About three thirty, the *Dannesborg* blew up with a roar, after grounding in flames near the Trekroner batteries.

Nelson decided to send a boat of truce ashore to stop the unnecessary slaughter. His letter was carefully written, as he stood at the casing of the rudder-head. The ship's purser copied the text. It read:

> TO THE BROTHERS OF ENGLISHMEN,
> THE DANES:
>
> Lord Nelson has directions to spare Denmark, when no longer resisting—but if the firing is continued on the part of Denmark, Lord Nelson will be obliged to set on fire all the floating-batteries he has taken, without having the power of saving the brave Danes who have defended them.
>
> Dated on board His Britannic Majesty's Ship *Elephant*, Copenhagen Roads, April 2nd, 1801.
>
> NELSON and BRONTË, Vice-Admiral,
> under the Command of
> Admiral Sir Hyde Parker.

The truce message was placed in an envelope, and the secretary was ready to seal it with a paste seal (wafer). Nelson stopped him, and asked that a candle and sealing wax be brought. The man sent for the candle was killed, and when this was reported to Nelson he asked for another messenger.

"May I take the liberty of asking," said Stewart, "why—under so hot a fire, and after so lamentable an accident, you have attached so much importance to a circumstance apparently so trifling?"

"Had I used the wafer," Nelson replied, "it would

still be wet when presented to the Crown Prince. He would have inferred that the letter was sent off in a hurry, and that we had some very pressing reasons for being in a hurry. The wax told no tales."

The message served its purpose. The Crown Prince agreed to allow Nelson to secure his prisoners and prizes, while both sides flew flags of truce. The Danish representative, General Adjutant Lindholm, was referred to Admiral Parker for any further negotiations.

"Your Lordship's motives for sending a flag of truce to our Government can never be misconstrued," wrote Lindholm to Nelson, "and your subsequent conduct has sufficiently shown that humanity is always the companion of true valor."

Sir Hyde Parker ignored the fact that Nelson had disobeyed his signal "39." As he had left the planning and fighting up to Nelson, he also decided to leave the later negotiations up to him.

On the day after the battle, Nelson went ashore to discuss the terms of peace with the Prince of Denmark. He wrote that he "Dined with him in the Palace and had two hours' conversation. At eight, returned on board the *London* to communicate the result of my business."

As a diplomat, Nelson proved his merit in breaking the Coalition of the Baltic States. The political gains were of great importance. It was a great victory, and trade was resumed with Denmark.

The Battle at Copenhagen was a valiant, though bloody, struggle. Nelson had never fought a fiercer battle, nor had he ever suffered such losses. Over 900 British were killed or wounded. The Danish casualties and prisoners numbered over 6,000.

When awards were granted, Nelson was raised in the peerage to a Viscount. Admiral Graves became a Knight of the Bath. Unfortunately, no other awards were made, either to the captains or their men, who had fought so bravely.

"Your Lordship's whole conduct," Lord St. Vincent wrote to Nelson, "from your first appointment to this hour, is the subject of constant admiration. It does not become me to make comparisons—all agree there is but one Nelson!"

After the Battle of Copenhagen, Mr. George Rose entered a record in his diary of a breakfast conversation he had with Lord St. Vincent:

"His Lordship, on the late glorious victory at Copenhagen, told me the merit of the attack rested solely with Lord Nelson—as Sir Hyde Parker had been decidedly adverse to the attempt being made, and was overruled only by the perseverance and firmness of the former.

"In the middle of the action Sir Hyde had made a signal for discontinuing the engagement. Lord St. Vincent then added: 'For these causes, we have recalled Sir Hyde, and Lord Nelson is to remain with the command.' "

Nelson shifted his flag back to the *St. George* shortly after the battle. On the fifth of May, he received word that he had been appointed Commander-in-chief in the Baltic. He then decided to see what the Russians were up to, and set sail for Reval.

Russia's belligerent attitude toward England came to an end when Czar Paul was murdered during the night of March 24. The new Sovereign, Alexander I, was a reasonable ruler and neutral toward England.

By the time Nelson arrived at Reval, the ice had melted, permitting the entire Russian squadron to sail to their base at Cronstadt.

Nelson received a letter stating that Emperor Alexander was displeased at the appearance of the British Fleet in a Russian port. It stressed that "no negotiation with your Court can take place, so long as a naval force is in sight of his ports."

A diplomatic reply was sent by Nelson.

"My conduct, I feel, is so entirely different to what your Excellency has expressed in your letter, that I have only to regret, that my desire to pay a marked attention to His Imperial Majesty has been so entirely misunderstood. That being the case, I shall sail immediately into the Baltic."

To crown Nelson's victory at Copenhagen, he received a rewarding reply. A most important sentence read: "His Imperial Majesty has ordered the immediate raising of the embargo placed upon the English merchant ships."

There was now little need for Nelson to remain in the Baltic. He asked repeatedly to be relieved of his command that he might return to England. Although his letters often mentioned his poor health at this time, his days were long and full. Colonel Stewart gave an interesting description of life on board Nelson's flagship.

"His hour of rising was four or five o'clock, and of going to rest about ten. Breakfast was never later than six, and generally nearer to five o'clock. A midshipman or two were always of the party, and I have known him to send during the middle watch [12 midnight to 4] to invite the little fellows to breakfast with him, when relieved.

"At the table with them, he would enter into their boyish jokes, and be the most youthful of the party. At dinner he invariably had every officer of the ship in their turn, and was both a polite and hospitable host.

"The whole ordinary business of the fleet was invariably despatched, as it had been by St. Vincent, before eight o'clock. The great command of time which Lord Nelson thus gave himself, and the alertness which this example imparted throughout the fleet, can only be understood by those who witnessed it."

Admiral Charles Pole relieved Nelson of his command in the Baltic on the nineteenth of June, and he sailed home to England in the brig *Kite.* Arriving at Yarmouth on the first of July, he went to the hospital to visit the wounded from the Battle of Copenhagen. Then he was able to spend a brief leave with the Hamiltons and Horatia.

Trouble came all too soon, from an old familiar source—Napoleon. Only eleven days after Nelson arrived home, Napoleon ordered a large massing of troops and gun boats at Boulogne for an invasion of England. News of this threat sent a chilling wave of fear throughout the country. It gave the people great confidence when their greatest naval hero was placed in command of an anti-invasion force between Orfordness and Beachy Head. On July 27, Nelson hoisted his flag in the frigate *L'Unite* at Sheerness.

This was actually dull duty for Nelson, for he spent most of his time pitching and rolling at anchor in various frigates, the *L'Unite*, *Medusa*, and the *Amazon.* Chilling winds built up the surf, and the small frigates rolled heavily in the open sea. Many of the men were seasick, and Nelson himself was no exception. He was so seasick, he wrote that "I cannot hold up my head."

The monotony of the invasion watch was broken in August by two British raids on Boulogne. The attempts to destroy the French flotilla there, however, were not successful. The boats were chained securely together, and they were heavily protected by shore batteries. The raids nevertheless showed Napoleon that Great Britain did not intend to sit idly by.

A very good friend of Nelson's, Commander Edward Parker, was killed in one of the raids. Nelson had always treated him as he would his own son, and grieved over his loss. Since the government did not pay any of Parker's expenses, Nelson assumed his entire debts, and medical and burial expenses. After the funeral ashore, Nelson wrote: "Thank God the dreadful scene is past. I scarcely know how I got over it."

Nelson's duty with the anti-invasion force seemed like an eternity, and he looked forward to returning to the house which he had asked Emma to buy.

"The weather is very bad," he wrote to Emma, "and I am very seasick. I cannot answer your letter properly—but I am writing a line, to get on shore, if possible. I entreat you to get the house and furniture. I will be so happy to lend it to you and Sir William."

The country place purchased by Lady Hamilton was called Merton, and during the miserable days of bobbing off shore in a frigate, Nelson longed for the comfort of his new home.

The Treaty of Amiens was signed on March 25, 1802. This brought peace with France, and made it possible for Nelson to haul down his flag and leave for home. On the tenth of April he went ashore, eagerly heading for Merton—the chief topic of his personal correspondence for months.

His letters to Emma had shown a lively interest in his country home.

"Have we a nice church at Merton?"—"I admire the pigs and poultry. Sheep are certainly most beneficial to eat the grass. I intend to have a farming book."—"I shall, you may rely, admire the pig-stye, ducks, fowls, etc., for everything you do, I look upon as perfect."—"I should have got well, long ago, in a warm room, with a good fire, and sincere friends."—"How I should laugh, to see you,—the beautiful Emma, rowing a one-armed Admiral in a boat!"

For Nelson, country living became a pleasant change from his seagoing life. Yet he could not completely forget the Navy. A grassy walkway came to be known as "the quarterdeck," and a stream running through the land was called "the Nile." Emma had placed many of his war trophies around the house, and life was generally pleasant.

During these months, Nelson often visited London, busying himself with affairs of Parliament and the Admiralty. He was particularly anxious to obtain recognition for his captains, officers, and men, who had fought so bravely at Copenhagen. However, he was unsuccessful in this. Many years after Nelson's death, the government finally recognized the valor of the men in the bloody battle, and awarded medals. By then, however, only one of his captains was still alive—Captain John Lawford of the *Polyphemus*, who was made a Knight of the Bath, thirty-seven years after the battle!

During the course of thirteen peaceful months at

Merton, Nelson concerned himself with a number of progressive public matters. He wrote a memorandum to the Prime Minister on forest conservation, suggesting that the oak trees in the Forest of Dean be cultivated and preserved. Doubtless Nelson had in mind the future supply of beams, boards, and masts for His Majesty's ships! He made suggestions to the Admiralty concerning plans for manning ships and improving the conditions of the seamen. He also proposed certificates of service to the men who served in the Navy, together with some compensation for their years of faithful service.

Peace with France was not destined to last very long, however. Napoleon's reasons for the treaty had not been designed for peace—but for war.

Great Britain resumed world trade, and relaxed after the many years of war. Napoleon, however, did not relax. He hoped that the temporary peace with Great Britain would give him time to build up his fleet of 200 ships-of-the-line. This would make him unbeatable. To accomplish this, Napoleon planned to build about twenty-five ships annually and increase his naval supplies and munitions.

In France the cry of "Liberté" had become a mockery. From the boiling pot of the Revolution, a cruel, tyrannical dictatorship had risen. Like other dictatorships in history, a free press without rigid control could not be allowed. The British, however, were free to call a spade a spade, and the journalists and cartoonists wasted no time in pricking Napoleon with the needle of wit and ridicule. Napoleon had the English periodicals read to him during his bath, and he would bang on the side of the tub with rage whenever a particularly pointed remark penetrated his thin dictatorial skin.

British officials had little sympathy for the plump little dictator whose lust and ego had brought death and suffering to so many thousands. Striking back through his own newspapers, Napoleon, reacting like a teased bull, exchanged insult for insult. This friction continued to build up, until it created an atmosphere for further hostilities.

Napoleon's next move was to pounce on Switzerland, grabbing an area that would give him a corridor into Italy through the high, winding Simplon pass. This capped a series of unforgivable breaches by the "hero of France." The British reaction was a fair protest which stated that Switzerland had the right to conduct her own affairs without a foreign country interfering. This threw Napoleon into a rage.

Speaking in the House of Lords on November 23, 1802, Nelson strongly defended the "traditional faith, honour, generous sympathies, and diplomatic influence of England."

Napoleon did not expect England to take so bold a stand against his international atrocities. He could not tolerate opposition or criticism. His temperament was bringing on a war before he was fully prepared for it.

Bonaparte's dockyards were busy, but they were nowhere near the goals he had set in reprovisioning after the years of blockade. The French shipbuilding yards had hardly started to build up his Navy.

Trouble overseas also plagued Napoleon. Much of his fleet was scattered around the world. Part of it was still at San Domingo in the West Indies, where his forces had smashed an uprising by overwhelming the Negro Republic. The French victory was costly, however, for 25,000 troops died of yellow fever.

Napoleon was not ready to wage the crushing war he planned against England. In his usual deceitful way, he proposed that France and England rule the world together. This proposal was completely unacceptable to England, for her ambition was to trade with the world, not to conquer it.

Again and again, Napoleon violated the peace terms. The fair-minded British could not stand for it any longer. Britain declared war on France on May 18, 1803. Bonaparte was enraged because the war he so surely provoked had come too soon. In his anger he ordered 10,000 British tourists in France arrested. This act of treachery convinced the British that they were dealing with an enemy with whom true peace was impossible.

"They want us to jump the ditch, and we will jump it!" Napoleon stated, referring to the English Channel.

The people of England were confident that they could defend themselves, and sang this popular ditty:

We'll shake hands and be friends.
If they won't, why, what then?
We'll send our brave Nelson
to thrash them again!

CHAPTER FIFTEEN

"SALT BEEF AND THE FRENCH FLEET"

Nelson's peaceful life at Merton was soon disturbed. Sir William Hamilton was failing fast, and on the sixth of April, 1803, he died in Emma's arms. In his will, Sir William mentioned Nelson as "the most virtuous, loyal, and truly brave character I have ever met."

War with France was imminent, and on May the sixteenth Nelson was appointed Commander-in-chief in the Mediterranean. Leaving Merton, he hurried to Spithead. There, on the eighteenth, he hoisted his flag on board the stately 100-gun HMS *Victory*.

Sailing from Portsmouth, the ship set course for a rendezvous with Admiral William Cornwallis off Brest, France. Nelson was ordered to turn his majestic flagship over to him, if the Admiral felt he needed it for the blockade of Brest.

After a two-day search, Cornwallis could not be located near the rendezvous point. Nelson, reluctant to lose a fine northerly wind, decided to shift to the frigate *Amphion*, and headed for the Mediterranean on the evening of the twenty-third. In his eagerness to get on station, Nelson gave up three spacious rooms which made up his luxurious quarters in the *Victory*. Instead, he sailed toward Gibraltar "with all the splendor of a convict—seven or eight sleeping in one cabin." On the eighth of July, he joined the fleet off Toulon.

The French Fleet was located at three ports—Brest, Cádiz, and Toulon. Sir William Cornwallis commanded the British Fleet blockading Brest, while Vice Admiral Cuthbert Collingwood's fleet sailed off Cádiz. Nelson's fleet was to watch Toulon, the Straits of Messina, and the approach to the Adriatic. Napoleon hoped to have his three fleets leave port, evade the British blockading ships, and join forces. This would give him control of the English Channel long enough to transport his army across it and invade England.

Admiral Cornwallis did not need the *Victory*, and at the end of July, the towering masts of his magnificent three-deck flagship hove into view. Thomas Hardy, one of his favorite Captains, was transferred from the *Amphion* to command the *Victory*. Nelson's Captain of the Fleet (Chief of Staff) was Rear Admiral George Murray. Dr. Alexander Scott served as the fleet chaplain, as well as Nelson's interpreter and translator. His secretary was John Scott. This group formed Nelson's "immediate family" during his years in the *Victory*.

For eighteen long months the French ships did not venture out of port. Nelson hoped to lure them out by keeping his main fleet out of sight, while his frigates kept a vigilant watch. The days went by with the constant load of heavy correspondence, the struggle for supplies, and convoying ships past the pirates along the African coast of the Mediterranean.

The central base of operations selected by Nelson for his fleet was in the shelter of the Maddalena Islands, off the northeast coast of Sardinia. There he could load provisions and casks of water for his ships at an anchorage where they could get underway at any time, regardless of the wind's direction.

Nelson was promoted to Vice Admiral of the White on the twenty-third of April, 1804. By the time the news arrived on board the *Victory*, however, it was July. His white flag was hoisted to the top of the mast on the thirty-first.

"Our days pass so much alike," Nelson wrote, "that, having described one, you have them all."

Dr. Gillespie, who had been on board the *Victory* for only a short while, recorded his daily routine:

"At six o'clock my servant brings a light and informs me of the hour, wind and weather, and course of the ship. I immediately dress and generally repair to the deck, the dawn at this season [October] and latitude being apparently at about half or three-quarters past six.

"Breakfast is announced in the Admiral's cabin, where Lord Nelson, Rear Admiral Murray, Captain Hardy, the chaplain, secretary, one or two officers of the ship, and your humble servant assemble and breakfast on tea, hot rolls, toast, cold tongue, etc. When finished, we repair upon deck to enjoy the majestic sight of the rising sun surmounting the smooth and placid waves of the Mediterranean, which supports the lofty and tremendous bulwarks [ships] of Britain, following in regular train their admiral in the *Victory*.

"Between the hours of seven and two there is plenty of time for business, study, writing, and exercise. At two o'clock, a band of music plays till within a quarter of three, when the drum beats the tune called 'The Roast Beef of Old England'—to announce the Admiral's dinner, which is served up exactly at three o'clock. It generally consists of three courses and a dessert of the choicest fruit, together with three or four of the best wines.

"If a person does not feel himself perfectly at his ease it must be his own fault, such is the urbanity and hospitality which reigns here—notwithstanding the numerous titles, the four orders of Knighthood worn by Lord Nelson, and the well-earned laurels which he has acquired. Coffee and liqueurs close the dinner about half-past four or five o'clock—after which the company generally walk the deck, where the band plays for nearly an hour.

"At six o'clock tea is announced. The company again assemble in the Admiral's cabin, where tea is served before seven o'clock. As we are inclined, the party continue to converse with his Lordship, who at this time generally unbends himself—though he is at all times as free from stiffness and pomp as a regard to proper dignity will admit, and is very communicative.

"At eight o'clock a rummer of punch, with cake or biscuit is served, soon after which we wish the Admiral a 'good night.' Such is the journal of a day at sea in fine, or at least moderate, weather—in which this floating castle goes through the water with the greatest imaginable steadiness."

Another of Nelson's officers wrote:

"He [Nelson] possessed such a wonderful activity of mind, as even prevented him from taking ordinary repose, seldom enjoying two hours of uninterrupted sleep. On several occasions he did not quit the deck during the whole night. At these times he took no pains to protect himself from the effects of wet, or the night air—wearing only a thin great coat.

"He has frequently, after having his clothes wet through with rain, refused to have them changed. He seldom wore boots, and was consequently very liable to have his feet wet."

Nelson patiently waited for the French Fleet to put to sea.

"The weather was very thick when I looked into Toulon," he wrote at the end of October, "but I believe a vice admiral has hoisted his flag. They now amuse themselves with night signals and, by the quantity of rockets and blue lights they show with every signal, they plainly mark their position. These gentlemen must soon be so perfect in theory that they will come to sea to put their knowledge into practice. Could I see that day it would make me happy!"

Lord St. Vincent had been relieved as First Lord of the Admiralty, and Lord Melville had replaced him. In November, Melville had assigned Sir John Orde an area of Nelson's command from Gibraltar to Cape Finisterre. Nelson was upset by the news, since this argumentative and vindictive admiral had caused him much trouble before. After his arrival, Orde loaded his ships with scarce supplies from Gibraltar

—supplies which Nelson needed so badly. Orde also disrupted communications with England, for Nelson's frigates had to pass through Admiral Orde's area and he would then send them elsewhere.

Nelson was inclined to strike his flag and return home when this senior nuisance was given an adjacent command. However, he received news which quickly put this out of his mind. On the nineteenth of January, 1805, the *Active* and *Seahorse,* his two frigates, approached his anchorage at Maddalena under full sail. They were flying the long-awaited signal: "The enemy is at sea!"

Two days before, Admiral Pierre Villeneuve had sent a division of ships out of Toulon to chase away the British lookout frigates. The frigates, however, managed to keep track of the French Fleet as they set out ahead of a storm in the Gulf of Lyons. The storm so badly damaged the French ships that Villeneuve decided to head back to Toulon. His crews were, in fact, more skilled in the art of staying in port than putting to sea in any kind of weather.

"My fleet looked well at Toulon," wrote Villeneuve, "but when the storm came on, things changed at once. The sailors were not used to storms—they lay in seasick heaps about the decks. It was impossible to work the ships, hence yardarms were broken and sails were carried away. Our losses resulted as much from clumsiness and inexperience, as from defects in the materials delivered by the arsenals."

Nelson was so anxious to engage the French that he set out on a vain search for Villeneuve's fleet. Nelson sailed as far as Alexandria, Egypt, without finding any trace of the enemy. When he learned that the

French had returned to Toulon after a storm, he wrote to Admiral Collingwood:

"Bonaparte has often made his boast that our fleet would be worn out by keeping the sea, and that his fleet was kept in order and increasing, by staying in port. He now finds, I fancy, if Emperors hear the truth, that his fleet suffers more in a night than ours in a year!"

Meanwhile, Spain had decided to join Napoleon and she declared war on England in December. Bonaparte planned to have his fleets from various French ports rendezvous in the West Indies. En route, Spanish ships from Cartagena and Cádiz were to join them. After landing troops, they would seize as many of the British Islands in the West Indies as possible. Then the combined French and Spanish Fleet of about forty ships were to sail to Boulogne, France. There they would embark Napoleon's invasion troops and, with a superior fleet, invade England.

Villeneuve was more fortunate on his next attempt to slip past the British lookout frigates. His fleet set out from Toulon on the thirtieth of March. They were not sighted until the next morning by the frigates *Active* and *Phoebe*. The *Phoebe* sailed off to report to Nelson, while the *Active* continued to track the enemy. During the night, the French picked up a fine breeze, and in the darkness opened the distance from the *Active*. By morning they were out of sight.

Admiral Villeneuve's ships sailed off Cartagena in the hope that the Spanish Fleet there would join him. However, the Spanish had not yet loaded ammunition, and the French Fleet of eighteen ships continued on past Gibraltar on the eighth of April. On the ninth, the French force, bound for Cádiz, sent Sir John Orde's squadron fleeing to the north. Orde could not be blamed for deciding not to fight such a superior fleet. However, he could hardly be forgiven for not leaving a lookout frigate or two in the area to keep track of Villeneuve's fleet.

On the nineteenth, Nelson learned from a merchant ship that the French Fleet had sailed past Gibraltar into the Atlantic. This was ten days after the French and Spanish ships at Cádiz had joined Villeneuve and sailed westward into the setting sun.

By the time Nelson's Fleet neared Gibraltar, the wind was dead set against him.

"I cannot get a fair wind," the tortured Admiral wrote, "or even a side wind. Dead foul!"

Nelson's ships were not able to sail closer into the wind than about seven points of the compass. Even a small well-handled sail boat cannot do better than head within four points into the wind when "close-hauled."

Today, it is difficult to appreciate how much the ships of Nelson's day were dependent on the wind. At the mercy of the winds and out of communication with the rest of the world, Nelson and his men had a hard time of it, from the seamen in the rigging to the admiral of the fleet.

At Tetuan, Morocco, Nelson decided to take advantage of the foul wind to load supplies, beef, and water for a long voyage. He anticipated a run to the West Indies and back. At Gibraltar the officers had hardly made the shore when a change in the wind caught Nelson's eye. A cannon boomed from the *Victory*, and the prep signal was hoisted for getting underway. On the eleventh of May, the winds which had bottled him inside the Mediterranean finally filled the sails and wafted his fleet out into the Atlantic. The long chase was on!

"It will not be supposed," Nelson wrote to the Admiralty, "I am on a party of pleasure, running after eighteen ships-of-the-line with ten, and that to the West Indies. Salt beef and the French Fleet is far preferable to roast beef and champagne without them!"

Nelson set sail in the *Victory*, accompanied by nine other ships—the *Conqueror*, *Canopus*, *Belle Isle*, *Donegal*, *Leviathan*, *Spencer*, *Tigre*, *Swiftsure*, and the *Superb*. The *Royal Sovereign* had been detached. His fleet also included three frigates, the *Amphion*, *Diana*, and *Amazon*.

With a fine trade wind behind them, Nelson's ships reached Barbados on the fourth of June. Near the West Indies two additional ships joined his fleet. He now had twelve sail-of-the-line.

The distance from the Straits of Gibraltar to the West Indies had been covered in slightly over three weeks—3,227 nautical miles of fine sailing under the ballooning canvas. The British ships gained ten days on the French Fleet, which had arrived at Martinique on the fourteenth of May.

Many of Admiral Villeneuve's men had fallen sick during their voyage; those who died were buried at sea. Upon arrival, a thousand more sick and dying men were taken ashore. Villeneuve was about to attack Barbados when he heard that Nelson had arrived there. He was so terrified at the thought of fighting Nelson, that he abandoned all further plans to seize the Islands of the British West Indies and immediately sailed for France!

Nelson, never lacking courage, would not have hesitated to attack the large combined fleet, although it now numbered twenty ships-of-the-line under Admirals Villeneuve and Gravina.

"Powerful as their force may be, they shall not with impunity make any great attacks. My fleet is compact, theirs must be unwieldy. Although a pretty fiddle, I don't believe that either Gravina or Villeneuve know how to play on it."

During his search for the French, Nelson received incorrect information; however, some of it was not too harmful. Nevertheless, a message from General Brereton, commanding the troops on Santa Lucia, informed him that the enemy ships had been sighted going southward on the night of May twenty-eighth.

Against his better judgment, Nelson sailed for Tobago and Trinidad, arriving there on the sixth of June. When he discovered that Brereton's information was false, he sailed back to Antigua. By then, the French and Spanish ships were northward of the West Indies, bound for France.

"But for wrong information," Nelson wrote, "I should have fought the battle on the sixth of June—I was assured that his [General Brereton's] information was very correct, but I must not despair."

Even though he was unsuccessful in catching the enemy fleet, Nelson had driven Villeneuve out of the West Indies. By doing so, he saved about 200 sugar ships from capture, and chased the enemy fleet from their rendezvous.

Hoping to catch them on their return voyage to Europe, Nelson set sail from Antigua on the thirteenth of June, heading northward to catch the steady easterly trade winds. Although Nelson gained on Villeneuve, his ships were still eight days behind the enemy upon reaching the Azores on the eighth of July.

Nelson's fear that Villeneuve may have returned to the West Indies ended when an American schooner was hailed. Her skipper confirmed that the French and Spanish ships were bound for Europe.

Nelson's Fleet anchored at Gibraltar on the nineteenth.

"No French Fleet, nor any information about them," he wrote.

When Nelson went ashore on the twentieth, it was the first time he had set foot on land in over two years!

On the twenty-second, the twenty French and Spanish ships encountered a British Fleet of fifteen, under Admiral Robert Calder. After Nelson's long chase to the West Indies, the big enemy fleet fell right into Sir Robert Calder's lap!

In hazy weather and the darkness of late afternoon, the ships engaged each other, using gun flashes as targets. During the brief battle, HMS *Windsor Castle* lost her mainmast, and two of the Spanish ships were captured. Although Calder claimed a victory, it was not the kind Nelson, nor the Admiralty, had looked forward to.

Aided by poor visibility, the enemy fleet sailed away undetected into Vigo Bay. After Calder lost track of them, he sent part of his fleet to blockade Rochefort. He then sailed with nine ships to join Cornwallis off Brest.

Nelson joined Cornwallis at Brest on the fifteenth

of August, where he left all his ships except the *Victory* and the *Superb*. These sailed for England and dropped anchor at Spithead on the eighteenth.

"At daylight weighed, working up to Spithead," Nelson wrote. "At nine anchored at Spithead—just two years and three months from my arrival [to embark] at Portsmouth."

After sailing over 12,000 nautical miles, the long chase after Villeneuve had come to an end.

Crowds gathered at every vantage point along the coast to welcome their hero home once more. Nelson's barge pulled ashore to the cheering of his countrymen. The merchants trading with the West Indies gave him their heartfelt thanks for saving their property from the enemy.

"I met Nelson in a mob in Piccadilly, and got hold of his arm," wrote Lord Minto, "so that I was mobbed too. It is really quite affecting to see the wonder and admiration—the love and respect of the whole world—and the genuine expression of all these sentiments at once, from the gentle and simple, the moment he is seen."

A hero's welcome and a brief stay at Merton were Nelson's rewards after his long chase. Surrounded by his family, his friends, and Emma, Nelson enjoyed the short leave of a sailor home from the sea.

CHAPTER SIXTEEN

"I WILL LAY DOWN MY LIFE IN THE ATTEMPT"

A carriage drawn by four horses rattled up the drive at Merton. It was five o'clock in the morning, the second of September, 1805. Captain Blackwood had arrived in the frigate *Euryalus* and was carrying dispatches from Admiral Collingwood. Bound for the Admiralty, he decided to stop first at Merton.

Always an early riser, Nelson was already up and about.

"I am sure you bring me news of the French and Spanish Fleets," Nelson remarked. "I think I shall yet have to beat them."

Nelson was right—Blackwood did have news about the combined French and Spanish Fleet. It had put into Cádiz with almost forty ships-of-the-line and 30,000 men. However, it was unlikely that the enemy could stay in port long with the limited supplies at Cádiz. The combined fleet was therefore expected to sail out of port soon. This would give Nelson the chance he had waited for so long.

"Depend on it, Blackwood," Nelson promised. "I shall yet give Mr. Villeneuve a drubbing!"

Napoleon's plans for invasion again were clearly frustrated by the British Fleet blockading Cádiz.

"Thank God a thousand times!" Admiral Radstock wrote, "that these Jack O'Lanterns are once more safely housed without having done the mischief which was most justly dreaded."

Nelson spent his last days on shore concentrating on a plan to destroy the French Fleet. In the meantime, the *Victory* was getting ready for sea. Lord Barham, the First Lord of the Admiralty, was completely won over by the dynamic Nelson. He promised him forty ships, and his choice of officers.

"Choose yourself, my Lord," Nelson replied. "The same spirit actuates the whole profession. You cannot choose wrong."

Honors enough for a dozen men had already been given to Nelson. He could have left the enemy fleets for others to conquer. However, the Admiralty and the British people would have none other than Nelson himself to lead the British Fleet into battle.

"I have much to lose and little to gain," wrote Nelson before he left Merton. "I go because it's right, and I will serve the country faithfully."

On the thirteenth of September, Emma said her last sad farewell to her loved one.

"Lady Hamilton was in tears all day," Lord Minto wrote. "She could not eat, and hardly drink, and near swooning, and all at the table."

That same evening, Nelson climbed into a carriage and, leaving Merton for what was to be the last time, drove off into the night. He did look back at "dear, dear Merton, where I left all which I hold dear in this world." Then looking ahead, he wrote during a change of horses, "May the great God whom I adore, enable me to fulfill the expectations of my country." Nelson had a premonition that he would never return.

The following morning at Portsmouth, he completed his business and personal affairs at the George Inn. That afternoon he walked down the boat landing and set out in his barge for the *Victory*. Crowds of people had assembled to see their hero leave. So many had gathered that they were hard to keep under control. As his barge shoved off, Nelson waved his hat at the cheering crowds.

"I had their huzzas before—now I have their hearts!" he remarked to Captain Hardy, as the men rhythmically rowed the barge toward the *Victory*.

On Sunday morning, the fifteenth, the men strained at the capstain bars as the ship's anchor was weighed. With Captain Blackwood's frigate *Euryalus*, the *Victory* sailed for the coast of Portugal.

Nelson arrived off Lisbon on the twenty-fifth, and asked the British Consul to keep his presence there a secret. He also sent word to Admiral Collingwood that, when the *Victory* joined the fleet, they were not to fire salutes or make any signals that might inform the enemy fleets of his arrival.

When the *Victory* finally joined the fleet, Nelson was enthusiastically greeted by everyone. The men in the ships were elated when they heard that they would be led into battle by Nelson. Morale in the fleet soared to a new high. The captains and admirals from other ships of the fleet were invited on board the *Victory* to dine with him. During these visits, Nelson explained his battle plan.

"The reception I met with on joining the fleet caused the sweetest sensation of my life. The officers who came on board to welcome my return forgot my rank as Commander-in-chief in the enthusiasm with which they greeted me," he wrote. "As soon as these emotions were past, I laid before them the plan I had previously arranged for attacking the enemy. It was not only my pleasure to find it generally approved, but clearly perceived and understood."

Captain George Duff of the *Mars* wrote about his visit on board the *Victory* with Nelson.

"I dined with his Lordship yesterday, and had a very merry dinner. He certainly is the pleasantest Admiral I ever served under. We all wish to do what he likes—without any kind of orders."

To Lady Hamilton, Nelson wrote: "I believe my arrival was most welcome, not only to the Commander of the Fleet [Collingwood], but also to every individual in it. When I came to explain to them the 'Nelson touch,' it was like an electric shock—all approved. 'It was new—it was singular—it was simple!' From Admirals downwards, it was repeated—'It must succeed, if ever they will allow us to get at them. You are, my Lord, surrounded by friends whom you inspire with confidence.' "

The day after he joined the fleet, Nelson observed his forty-seventh birthday on the twenty-ninth of September. The enthusiastic reception given him was his most appreciated gift.

One unpleasant task fell to Nelson upon joining the fleet. He was to advise Sir Robert Calder that the Admiralty was dissatisfied with his battle with Admiral Villeneuve's fleet in July. They felt that Calder should have followed up his encounter with the enemy, or at least kept track of where they were sailing.

Calder had been jealous of Nelson's bold initiative ever since the Battle off Cape St. Vincent. However, Nelson felt no animosity toward him, and wrote to the Admiralty: "It will give your Lordship pleasure to find, as it has me, that an inquiry is what the Vice Admiral wishes. Sir Robert thinks that he can clearly prove that it was not in his power to bring the combined squadrons to battle."

In a more intimate letter to Emma, he wrote, "I have had, as you will believe, a very distressing scene with poor Sir Robert Calder. He has written home to beg an inquiry, feeling confident that he can fully justify himself. I sincerely hope he may, but I have given him the advice as to my dearest friend. He is in adversity, and if he ever has been my enemy, he now feels the pang of it, and finds me one of his best friends."

Nelson decided to grant Calder's wish to sail back to England in his flagship, the *Prince of Wales*, even though her ninety guns would be needed in a battle with a superior fleet. Realizing that his compassion overruled his better judgment, Nelson wrote the Admiralty: "I much fear I shall incur the censure of the Board, but I trust that I shall be considered to have done right as a man to a brother officer in affliction."

Nelson's battle plan had been revolving in his mind even before he left Merton. The long-accepted tradition of a sea battle had been two parallel lines of ships blazing away at each other—until one line battered the other into submission.

"Rodney broke the enemy's line in one place—I will break it in two."

This was Nelson's plan at the Battle of Trafalgar. Two columns of British ships, one led by Collingwood, the other by Nelson, would pierce the long battle line of the combined French and Spanish Fleet.

To lure the enemy fleet out of Cádiz, Nelson placed his battle ships far out at sea where they would be out of sight over the horizon. Captain Henry Blackwood was placed in charge of the inshore lookout frigates.

"I am convinced that you estimate as I do," Nelson told Blackwood, "the importance of not letting these rogues escape us without a fair fight!"

The frigates kept a close-in watch on the port, with a system of relaying signals by night and day. If the enemy ships came out during daylight hours, the frigates were to fire guns every three minutes. If at night, rockets were to be fired from the masthead.

"I rely on you, that we can't miss getting hold of them," Nelson told Blackwood. "I will give them such a shaking as they never yet experienced—at least I will lay down my life in the attempt."

One day while waiting to engage the enemy, the *Victory* sent a signal to the fleet that a ship was about to sail for England with mail. All ships were to have their mail bags ready for pickup. The mail was loaded on board, and the ship headed northward under full sail.

A midshipman, talking to Lieutenant Pasco, said something to the lieutenant which obviously made him angry. Noting this, Nelson asked what was wrong.

"Nothing that need trouble your Lordship."

"You are not the man to lose your temper for nothing."

"Well, if you must know, my Lord, I will tell you. You see that cockswain? We have not a better man on board the *Victory*. I was told that he was so busy receiving and getting off mail bags, that he forgot to drop his own letter to his wife into them. He has just discovered it in his own pocket!"

"Hoist a signal to bring her [the ship] back; who knows that he may fall in action tomorrow. His letter shall go with the rest!"

This was the kind of consideration Nelson had for his enlisted men that made them idolize him and follow him willingly into battle.

On the thirteenth of October, two old friends—a ship and a captain—sailed over the horizon to join the fleet. It was Captain Edward Berry in the *Agamemnon*. When his arrival was reported to Nelson, the Admiral cheerfully remarked: "Here comes Berry! Now we shall have a battle!"

Captain Berry had seen more battle action than any captain in the British Navy. He was soon to see another—his luck in bringing enemy action still held!

On the morning of October nineteenth, the enemy ships sailed out of the port of Cádiz on an easterly wind. Sighted by Blackwood's frigates, the signal was sent from masthead to masthead until it reached the *Victory*, fifty miles at sea.

"The Enemy Fleet is at Sea!"

"The signal has been made that the enemy's combined fleet are coming out of port," read Nelson's last letter to Emma. "We have very little wind, so that I have no hopes of seeing them before tomorrow. May

God Almighty give us success over these fellows, and enable us to get a peace."

During the day, the wind died down and only twelve enemy ships had cleared port. On the morning of the twentieth, the rest of the combined fleet sailed out, one after the other. By mid-afternoon, a total of thirty-three French and Spanish ships-of-the-line were at sea.

As the haze of morning cleared away in the afternoon, Blackwood was able to pass accurate information on to Nelson, who spent most of the day pacing the *Victory*'s poop deck. Since a night battle was impractical for such a large clash between the two fleets, Nelson planned his attack for the following morning.

"Tomorrow I will do that which will give you younger gentlemen something to talk and think about for the rest of your lives," Nelson remarked at the dinner table, "but I shall not live to know about it myself."

In the early morning light of the twenty-first, the combined French and Spanish Fleet were outlined against the sky, with the dim shape of Cape Trafalgar barely visible beyond.

Shortly after six o'clock, Nelson sent out a signal to form two columns. The wind was light and the enemy still twenty miles away. Sailing on a southerly course, the combined fleet was heading for the Straits of Gibraltar.

The British Fleet sailed on a northerly course. Nelson wanted to make sure that they advanced far enough so they could not retreat back to Cádiz. At the same time, he wanted to engage them early in the day in order to win a decisive victory before dark. Six hours were to pass before the two fleets joined in battle.

Few signals were necessary, for all the admirals and captains knew the general plan. Nelson signaled to *"Form the order of sailing"* and to *"Prepare for Battle."*

The British Fleet (twenty-seven ships-of-the-line, four frigates, a cutter, and a schooner) then sailed eastward toward Cape Trafalgar. They formed two crooked lines, sailing the best they could in the light breeze. Among their twenty-seven ships-of-the-line were seven 3-deck ships with 90 to 100 guns, one 80-gun ship, sixteen 74's, and three 64's.

Vice Admiral Nelson, the Commander-in-chief, headed one line of eleven ships. Following the *Victory* were the *Téméraire*, *Neptune*, *Conqueror*, *Leviathan*, *Britannia*, *Ajax*, *Orion*, *Agamemnon*, *Minotaur*, and the *Spartiate.*

Vice Admiral Collingwood in the *Royal Sovereign* lead the other line of fourteen ships—the *Belleisle*, *Mars*, *Tonnant*, *Bellerophon*, *Colossus*, *Achille*, *Revenge*, *Defiance*, *Polyphemus*, *Dreadnought*, *Swiftsure*, *Thunderer*, and the *Defence.*

The *Prince* sailed in between the two lines. The twenty-seventh British ship, the *Africa*, missed a signal and sailed out of touch with the main fleet during the night. She was to the north and was making her best speed to rejoin.

The French Admiral, Villeneuve, commanded the Combined Fleet (eighteen French and fifteen Spanish ships-of-the-line, five French frigates, and two brigs). Spanish Admiral Gravina was second in command.

Ranging from north to south were the *Neptuno* (Spanish), *Scipion* (French), *Intrépide* (Fr.), *Formidable* (Fr.), *Duguay Trouin* (Fr.), *Mont Blanc* (Fr.), *Rayo* (Sp.), *San Francisco de Asís* (Sp.), *San Augustin* (Sp.), *Héros* (Fr.), *Santissima Trinidad* (Sp.), *Bucentaure* (Fr.), *Redoubtable* (Fr.), *San Justo* (Sp.), *Neptune* (Fr.), *San Leandro* (Sp.), *Santa Ana* (Sp.), *Indomptable* (Fr.), *Fougueux* (Fr.), *Monarca* (Sp.), *Pluton* (Fr.), *Algeciras* (Fr.), *Bahama* (Sp.), *Aigle* (Fr.), *Swiftsure* (Fr.), *Montañez* (Sp.), *Argonaute* (Fr.), *San Ildefonso* (Sp.), *Argonauta* (Sp.), *Achille* (Fr.), *Príncipe de Asturias* (Sp.), *Berwick* (Fr.), and *San Juan de Nepomuceno* (Sp.).

The huge *Santissima Trinidad* mounted 130 guns, and three others had 100 or more guns. There were six 80-gun ships, one with 64 guns, and the rest were 74-gun ships.

Midshipman Badcock, serving in HMS *Neptune*, described the enemy line as the British approached.

"It was a beautiful sight when their line was completed, their broadsides turned towards us, showing their iron teeth—now and then trying the range of a shot to ascertain the distance that they might, the moment we came within point blank [about 600 yards], open their fire upon our van ships—no doubt with the hope of dismasting some of our leading vessels before they could close and break their line.

"Some of the enemy ships were painted like ourselves, with double yellow sides, some with a broad single red or yellow streak, others all black. The noble *Santissima Trinidad*, with four distinct lines of red, with a white ribbon between them, made her seem a superb man-of-war, which indeed she was! Her appearance was imposing, her figurehead splendidly ornamented with a colossal group of figures, painted white, representing the Holy Trinity from which she took her name."

Before the battle, Nelson decided to add a codicil to his will, in which he wrote: "I leave Emma Hamilton a legacy to my King and Country, that they will give her an ample provision to maintain her rank in life. I also leave to the beneficence of my Country my adopted daughter, Horatia."

He also went down to his cabin to write his now-famous prayer:

> May the Great God whom I worship, grant to my Country, and for the benefit of Europe in general, a great and glorious Victory—and may no misconduct in anyone tarnish it—and may humanity after Victory be the predominant feature in the British Fleet.
>
> For myself individually, I commit my life to Him who made me, and may His blessing light upon my endeavours for serving my Country faithfully. To Him I resign myself, and the just cause which is entrusted me to defend.
>
> Amen, Amen, Amen.

About seven in the morning, the French and Spanish Fleet wore around and sailed northward. Admiral Villeneuve abandoned his plan of heading for the Straits of Gibraltar, and resigned himself to the inevitable battle.

Amazingly, Admiral Villeneuve had guessed what Nelson's plan might be, and instructed his captains: "He will try to double our rear, cut through the line, and bring against the ships thus isolated groups of his own, to surround and capture them. Captains must rely on their courage and love of glory, rather than upon the signals of the Admiral, who may already be engaged and wrapped in smoke. The captain who is not engaged is not at his post."

Early that morning Nelson had called the captains of his frigates on board—Blackwood of the *Euryalus*, Thomas Capel of the *Phoebe*, Dundas of the *Naiad*, and Prowse of the *Sirius*. About nine o'clock, they made a tour of the *Victory*. Nelson wore his weather-beaten Admiral's frock coat, with his four colorful stars (showing his Orders) sewed on the left side.

As he walked along the decks he cut a heroic figure which could not fail to inspire his men, who already idolized him. Stopping, he reminded one of the powder passers to remove his shirt, so a spark would not set it on fire. It was a personal touch—a "Nelson touch"—which showed that he cared about his men.

When he reached the poop deck, he stopped for a moment to look down at the men on the weather deck. The crew immediately broke out into a spontaneous cheer. Nelson must have wondered how many of them would see another dawn.

The *Victory* and the *Royal Sovereign* slowly closed the long enemy line of towering masts and colorful ships. Nelson paced the quarterdeck with Captain Blackwood. Hardy was busy making "all possible sail" in the slackening wind.

Walking over to Pasco, his Signal Lieutenant, Nelson said to him:

"I wish to say to the fleet—'*England confides that every man will do his duty.*' You must be quick, for I have one more signal to make which is for '*Close Action.*' "

Pasco suggested the word "expects" in place of "confides" because it was already in the signal code, and would not have to be spelled out. The signal for *"Close Action"* was then hoisted to the topgallant masthead of the *Victory*.

"There it remained until shot away," Lieutenant Pasco later recorded.

Before the battle started, the frigate captains returned to their ships. Blackwood turned to Nelson as he left: "I trust, my Lord, that on my return to the *Victory*, I shall find your Lordship well, and in possession of twenty prizes."

"God bless you, Blackwood," the Admiral replied. "I shall never speak to you again."

The words were a prophecy, but there was little time to ponder their meaning. The first shot from the French ship *Fougueux* splashed in front of the *Royal Sovereign*, sending up a plume of water. This signaled the beginning of the battle, at high noon. Battle colors in all the ships were then hoisted—the national colors, and the admirals' flags.

Admiral Collingwood nonchalantly munched an apple as he paced the quarterdeck of the *Royal Sovereign*, and studied the ships of the enemy line. Collingwood's ships had always displayed superb gunnery. The men in his previous flagship, the *Dreadnought*, could fire her guns at an admirable rate of speed. The *Royal Sovereign*, in the short time she had been with the fleet, had made great progress in gunnery, and was sure to prove herself in battle.

"Now gentlemen, let us do something today which the world may talk of hereafter," he said to the officers around him.

Leading the lee division, Collingwood was closer to

the enemy line than Nelson was in the *Victory*, and he engaged the enemy first. The *Royal Sovereign* sailed on without firing, for ten minutes after the first shot from the *Fougueux*. As she drew closer to the *Fougueux*, Collingwood turned to his flag captain and remarked: "Rotherham, what would Nelson give to be here!"

The pell-mell struggle planned by Nelson and predicted by Villeneuve developed soon after the first shots were exchanged. From the *Victory*, Nelson watched Collingwood sail the *Royal Sovereign* through a hail of shot during the critical approach, when the enemy's broadsides had the advantage. Nelson had seen his courageous friend in battle before.

"See how that noble fellow Collingwood carries his ship into action!"

The *Royal Sovereign*, cutting across the bow of the *Fougueux*, hammered her with a devastating broadside. As the two ships swung around parallel to each other, they were so close that their muzzles were almost touching. The flash of fire from the muzzles of their cannon blackened the paint on the ships' sides. The French ship *Indomptable* ranged up on the other side of the *Royal Sovereign*, forcing her to fire port and starboard broadsides as fast as her gun crews could load and fire.

The *Belleisle* and the *Mars* soon arrived to support their flagship. Within fifteen minutes, eight ships of Collingwood's line had opened fire, joining the rumble and din of battle.

The *Africa*, approaching from the north, headed for the van of the enemy line. The daring 64-gun ship, under Captain Henry Digby, took on the big ships, and threw the enemy van into confusion. She sailed down the line with guns blazing. They could not figure out how the *Africa* fitted into the battle plan. Neither could anyone else! However, the ship fought a most admirable battle—a David among Goliaths!

Nelson and his men in the *Victory* had little time to watch the battle now in progress. Admiral Villeneuve's flagship, the *Bucentaure*, sailed within ranged of the *Victory*, and opened fire at 12:20. The first shot fell short. The second splashed alongside. The next few sailed over the top of the ship, and the battle gathered momentum. In a short time the long enemy line was again broken by the *Victory*, resulting in clusters of ships scrambling for positions, and blazing away at close range.

The *Victory* faced the broadsides of the *Bucentaure* as she approached, without being able to fire in return. The *Victory* also drew the fire of several other enemy ships. Cannon-balls ripped through her sails and swept away her studding-sail booms. She slowly lost speed as part of her canvas fell overboard into the water.

John Scott, Nelson's secretary, was killed instantly, as he stood talking to Captain Hardy. A round shot cut him almost in two.

"Is that poor Scott?" Nelson exclaimed.

In short order, the *Victory*'s mizzen topmast was shot off, and the ship's wheel was shattered. A shot crashed through the ship's side, and hurtled between Nelson and Hardy. As it struck a heavy block of timber, it sent out a burst of splinters. One of the fragments hit Hardy's foot, and carried away the buckle from his shoe. Nelson looked at him with a smile: "This is too warm work, Hardy, to last long!"

A cannon-shot plowed into a group of marines standing in formation on the poop deck, and killed eight of them. Nelson ordered the remaining marines to disperse so they wouldn't make such a choice target. Nelson himself was warned that his conspicuous coat made too good a target. He brushed this warning aside, however—there was no time to go below to change.

The guns of the *Victory* finally had a chance to open fire when she crossed the stern of the *Bucentaure*. From a point-blank range of ten yards, and with her yardarms brushing past the *Bucentaure*'s rigging, the *Victory*'s carronade blasted into the cabin windows of the stern gallery. Double-shotted broadside guns fired into the stern as they passed. Clouds of smoke and dust rolled back onto the *Victory*. Twenty guns and about four hundred men were put out of action on the French ship.

The *Bucentaure* was left behind, as the *Victory* sailed ahead toward the French *Neptune* and *Redoubtable*. Both ships had been thundering away at the *Victory*. Hardy asked which ship he should run down.

"It does not matter which we run on board of," Nelson replied. "Take your choice!"

Hardy set course for the 74-gun *Redoubtable*. About 1:15 the two ships collided, and the *Victory*'s yardarms snagged in the rigging of the French ship.

Astern of the *Victory* were Captain Eliab Harvey in the *Téméraire*, and Captain Thomas Fremantle in the *Neptune*. Behind them in close succession followed other ships of Nelson's column, the *Leviathan, Conqueror, Britannia, Ajax, Orion, and the Agamemnon.*

The thunder of cannon, the flash of flame, and huge clouds of smoke engulfed the battling ships. Locked in a duel with the *Redoubtable*, the *Victory* blazed away, shot for shot, with one of the best fighting ships of the enemy fleet.

Captain Lucas of the *Redoubtable* wrote: "I had 100 carbines fitted with long bayonets on board. The men to whom these were served out were so well accustomed to their use that they climbed half-way up the shrouds to open musketry fire. All those armed with swords were given broadsword practice every day, and pistols became familiar weapons to them."

Second Lieutenant Rotely of the Marine detachment on board the *Victory* later described the bloody battle.

"The poop deck became a slaughter-house, and soon after the commencement of the battle the two senior Lieutenants of Marines and half the original party were casualties.

"I was now on the middle deck. We were engaging on both sides—every gun was going off. A man should witness a battle in a three-decker from the middle deck, for it beggars all description! It bewilders the senses of sight and hearing.

"There was the fire from above, the fire from below, besides the fire from the deck I was upon—the guns recoiling with violence, reports louder than thunder, the decks heaving, and the sides straining. I fancied myself in the infernal regions, where every man appeared a devil. Lips might move, but orders and hearing were out of the question—everything was done by signs.

"The battle now raged at its greatest height. The *Redoubtable* had fallen on board us on our starboard side, and the soldiers from their tops were picking off our officers and men with deadly aim. We were also engaged with the *Santissima Trinidad* and the *Bucentaure*—though at a greater distance on our larboard [port].

"The reinforcement arrived at a most critical moment. Captain Adair's party [marines] was reduced to less than ten men, himself wounded in the forehead by splinters, yet still using his musket with effect. One of his last orders to me was: 'Rotely, fire away as fast as you can!' A ball struck him on the back of the neck and he was a corpse in a moment.

"At the same time our revered Chief [Nelson] fell, having received his mortal wound from a soldier in the mizzen top of the *Redoubtable.* The marines became exasperated. I was now in command [of them], and the first order I gave was to clear the mizzen top. Every musket was levelled at that top, and in five minutes not a man was left alive in it."

Lord Nelson and Captain Hardy had been pacing back and forth on the quarterdeck, between the wheel and the hatch leading below. It was then about 1:30. As they reached a turning point, Nelson fell. Hardy dropped down by his side, hoping that he was not badly wounded.

"They have done for me at last, Hardy. My backbone is shot through."

A sharpshooter had fired his musket from fifty

feet above in the *Redoubtable*'s mizzen top. It struck Nelson's left epaulette, punctured a lung, and pierced his spine. As Nelson was carried below, he covered his face with a handkerchief—he did not want his men to know that he had fallen.

Carried down into the cockpit with the rest of the wounded, Nelson's handkerchief fell from his face. The surgeon, Beatty, hurried over to his side.

"You can do nothing for me, Beatty. I have but a short time to live."

All around the din of battle continued, as Nelson bravely bled to death.

The *Victory* and the *Redoubtable* were still locked together. Both ships were fighting with great spirit and courage. HMS *Téméraire* sailed along at a favorable angle, and fired a devastating broadside into the *Redoubtable*.

"It would be difficult to describe the horrible carnage caused by the murderous broadside," Captain Lucas recorded. "More than 200 of our brave lads were killed or wounded. Our ship was so riddled that she seemed to be no more than a mass of wreckage.

"In this state the *Téméraire* hailed us to strike, and not prolong a useless resistance. I ordered several soldiers who were near me to answer this summons with musket shots, which was performed with the greatest zeal. At the very same minute the mainmast fell athwart the *Téméraire*, and that vessel's two topmasts fell on board the *Redoubtable*."

The French ship had proven a worthy opponent for the British flagship, but she finally struck her flag. "All our decks were covered with dead, buried beneath the debris, and the splinters from the different parts of the ship," Captain Lucas later recorded. "Out of the ship's company of 643 men we had 522 disabled—300 being killed and 222 wounded."

During the fierce fighting, many brave men were killed, and the ships shattered. As the battle drew to a close, the *Victory*, *Redoubtable*, and the *Téméraire* were ensnarled in their wrecked rigging. The *Fougueux,* battered to a hulk, drifted out of control into the general tangle.

Before Admiral Villeneuve's flagship *Bucentaure* surrendered, a signal was hoisted to the ten ships in the lead—to return, and take positions to engage the enemy. The ships, under Admiral Dumanoir, turned around. Five of them, fresh and undamaged, sailed near the blood-soaked decks of the *Victory*. Hardy was preparing to counter this new threat.

Nelson lingered on in his struggle against death while the last of the battle raged. Hardy had been too busy to leave the quarterdeck for a moment. The *Victory* finally broke clear of the tangled clutter of ships about 2:15 that afternoon, hardly able to maneuver.

Realizing that he was dying, Nelson called for Hardy. Midshipman Bulkeley quickly ran up to the quarterdeck to inform Hardy that Lord Nelson wanted to speak to him. When he returned, he told Nelson that, "circumstances required the captain's presence on deck," but that he would take the first favorable moment to visit his Lordship.

When Hardy had a chance, he went below to see Nelson. The old friends shook hands, and Doctor Beatty recorded the scene.

"Well, Hardy—how goes the battle? How goes the day with us?"

"Very well, my Lord. We have got twelve or fourteen of the enemy's ships in our possession, but five of their van have tacked, and show an intention of bearing down upon the *Victory*. I have called two or three of our fresh ships round us, and have no doubt of giving them a drubbing."

"I hope none of *our* ships have struck, Hardy?"

"No, my Lord! There is no fear of that."

"I am a dead man, Hardy. I am going fast. It will be all over with me soon."

Hardy expressed hope that Nelson might live.

"Oh no! It is impossible. My back is shot through. Beatty will tell you so."

Hardy hurried topsides to the quarterdeck to check the situation. The five enemy ships were sailing toward the *Victory*. HMS *Minotaur* and HMS *Spartiate,* the last two ships in Nelson's column, were arriving just in time. They had been almost becalmed in the light breeze, but succeeded in cutting across the bows of Dumanoir's ships, blasting them as they passed.

The two British ships took up positions between the *Victory* and the five enemy ships. Dumanoir then decided to sail on down the line, to support the ships tangling with Collingwood's column.

Hardy again returned belowdecks, and found Nelson much weaker, though still conscious. Hardy congratulated him on a brilliant victory, and reported that fourteen or fifteen enemy ships had been captured.

"That is well. I bargained for twenty." Realizing that the light winds and the ocean swells rolling in from the westward were warnings of an approaching storm, Nelson added: "Anchor, Hardy, anchor!" This order proved to be good advice, for many of the disabled ships were later in danger of being driven by the storm into the shore off Cape Trafalgar.

At the end, Doctor Scott attended Nelson, whose thoughts were again on the loved ones he had left behind forever.

"Take care of my dear Lady Hamilton, Hardy. Remember that I leave Lady Hamilton and my daughter Horatia as a legacy to my country."

As the last distant guns boomed off Trafalgar, Nelson half whispered, "Thank God, I have done my duty." He murmured, "God and my Country."

The great Lord Nelson was dead.

CHAPTER SEVENTEEN

"THE HERO WHO IN THE MOMENT OF VICTORY FELL—COVERED WITH IMMORTAL GLORY"

As the rising wind cleared the smoke of battle, the wreckage of many once-beautiful ships appeared. The storm, expected earlier in the day, was approaching fast. The exhausted men frantically tried to patch up leaking hulls, and hoist the tattered sails to the splintered masts.

The most spectacular sight after the battle was the French ship *Achille*—ablaze from bow to stern.

"The conclusion was grand beyond description—eighteen hulks of the enemy lying amongst the British Fleet without a stick [mast] standing, and the French *Achille* burning," Collingwood wrote to his old friend Sir Peter Parker.

Jeanette, the wife of one of the *Achille*'s crewmen, had been passing powder in the passageway leading to the forward magazine. The ship was a wreck, and a last full broadside from the *Prince* set her afire. Most of her crew were strewn around the decks in bloody disarray, and the remaining few could not begin to cope with the blaze.

As the booming of her guns stopped, the fire spread throughout the ship. Jeanette, choking from the smoke, hurried up to the gun deck to find her husband among the mangled bodies and the debris. Overhead, the flames crackled, and the heat was becoming intense. As the decks and beams burned, the heavy guns from the deck above crashed through, along with the flaming planks.

Not able to get topsides, she ran aft and climbed through the gun compartment port, where she could reach the chains leading to the rudder. Climbing out onto the back of the rudder, she hoped the ship would blow up, and end her misery!

The heat from the blaze began to melt the lead lining of the rudder trunk, and the molten lead started to drip on her. Leaping into the water, she grabbed a piece of cork. While she was struggling to stay afloat, another survivor pushed a plank toward her.

Jeanette was rescued by a boat from HMS *Pickle,* and taken aboard the *Revenge.* She was grateful when the British officers treated her as a "guest." One of them gave up his cabin, and money was collected to provide for her when she landed at Gibraltar. There, she happily found her husband among the survivors!

First Lieutenant W. Pryce Cumby of the *Bellerophon* wrote how he, and undoubtedly many others in the British Fleet, first learned of Nelson's death.

"At half past seven we observed the *Euryalus,* to which ship we knew Admiral Collingwood had shifted his flag, carried the lights of the Commander-in-chief. There were no [admiral's] lights on board the *Victory*—from which we were left to draw the melancholy inference that our gallant, our beloved Chief, the incomparable Nelson, had fallen."

The British sailors, who had fought so hard for victory, struggled just as hard to save the eighteen captured ships. Prize money was badly needed in their underpaid existence. Many of the prize ships were in such unseaworthy condition that they could not weather the storm, and had to be burned or blown up. As ships were destroyed, prisoners and wounded had to be transferred. Rough seas and strong winds added to their difficult job.

"I can only say that in my life I never saw such exertions as were made to save those ships, and would rather fight another battle, than pass such a week as followed it!" wrote Admiral Collingwood.

The men regretted the destruction of their prize ships—especially the loss of the valuable *Santissima Trinidad*! The beautiful four-decker, built of cedar, was the largest warship in the world—a masterpiece of shipbuilding. Among those rescued from the ship was a pet cat, and a pug dog! Captain Fremantle in HMS *Neptune* acquired the dog, and became very attached to his new pet.

"Admiral Villeneuve [then a prisoner] was with me on board over two days," he wrote to his wife Betsy. "I found him a very pleasant and gentleman-like man. The poor man was very low.

"I still have the pleasure of feeding and accommodating his captain, two aide-de-camps, and his adjutant general—who are true Frenchmen, but with whom I am much amused. I have also found an excellent French cook, and a true Spanish pug dog. These Frenchmen make me laugh at their accounts of Bonaparte, the Palais Royal, Paris, etc. The French captain drinks your health every day at dinner."

Collingwood, coping with dozens of crippled ships and hundreds of wounded, did a sterling job of tying up all the loose ends after the battle. One of the "loose ends" was Admiral Dumanoir's squadron of four ships. They were still a threat, their whereabouts being unknown.

Captain Thomas Baker in the frigate *Phoenix* sighted the four ships on the second of November. Pursued by the French, Baker headed straight for his planned rendezvous with Sir Richard Strachan's squadron, off Finisterre. Sir Richard, in HMS *Caesar,* had three other ships-of-the-line. On the morning of the fourth, the British and French fought a lively battle.

"The French squadron fought to admiration," Strachan wrote, "and did not surrender until their ships were unmanageable."

By nightfall, they struck their colors. All the ships of the great combined enemy fleet which had escaped into Cádiz were now accounted for, except the eleven ships under Admiral Gravina.

Lieutenant Lapenotiere, in the little schooner *Pickle,* sailed to England with news of the great victory at Trafalgar. He landed at Falmouth on the fifth of November, and immediately left for London. It was an hour after midnight when the Secretary of the Admiralty heard the rumble of carriage wheels in the courtyard below his office. He was still hard at work. The Lieutenant hurried up the stairs and into his office.

"Sir, we have gained a great victory—but we have lost Lord Nelson!"

Admiral Barham, the First Lord of the Admiralty, was awakened at once. All available clerks were soon at work preparing many messages, including those for the King, the Prime Minister, and the London Gazette.

When the King heard the astonishing news, he was absolutely speechless. Strangers stopped each other on the streets, shopkeepers and customers exchanged the news, and horsemen and coach drivers spread the word along the highways, and to the distant towns. The mixture of joy over the victory, and grief over Nelson's death, shocked the entire country from the King at Windsor Castle to the beggars on the streets of London—and from the highest to the lowest in the Fleet.

"I never set eyes on him," wrote a sailor from the *Royal Sovereign*, "for which I am both sorry and glad. To be sure I should like to have seen him, but then, all the men in our ship who have seen him are such soft toads, they have done nothing but blast their eyes ever since he was killed. Chaps that fought like the devil—sit down and cry like a wench!"

"I have not only to lament the fall of my Commander-in-chief," Collingwood wrote, "and the loss of a hero whose name will be immortal, and his memory ever dear to his country—but my heart is rent with most poignant grief for the death of a friend."

The *Euryalus* had been chosen by Collingwood to carry Nelson home to England. When the men in the *Victory* found out, they objected strenuously!

"The noble Admiral had fought with them, and fell upon their own deck," one of the petty officers remarked. "If, being put aboard a frigate, his body should fall into the hands of the enemy, it would make their loss doubly grievous to them. They were one and all resolved to carry it safely to England, or go to the bottom with it themselves."

Collingwood, hearing of the crew's devotion, was deeply impressed, and ordered Nelson returned in his own flagship. After repairs were made at Gibraltar, the *Victory* sailed for England on Nelson's final voyage.

The funeral at St. Paul's Cathedral, on the ninth of January, 1806, was one of the most impressive ceremonies England had ever seen. The King's ministers, six of the royal dukes, and the Prince of Wales were near the head of the procession. Over thirty admirals, more than one hundred naval captains, regiments of foot soldiers, cavalry, and artillery streamed by. Forty-eight seamen and marines from the *Victory,* wearing black neckerchiefs and stockings, impressed the crowds most of all. The coffin made from the mainmast of *L'Orient* was used as Nelson had planned.

Glory and victory crowned Lord Nelson's death. Napoleon's navy never did recover from its defeat at Trafalgar. His later conquests turned toward the land. It was on land that he was finally defeated by

Lord Wellington at Waterloo—ten years after the Battle of Trafalgar.

Today, at Portsmouth, England, history is brought to life. A visitor can walk the decks of the proud *Victory*, and almost hear the thunder of cannon. On the *Victory*'s deck is the very spot where "the hero who in the moment of victory fell—covered with immortal glory."

And the stately ships go on
To their haven under the hill;
But O for the touch of a vanished hand,
And the sound of a voice that is still!

Tennyson

Chronology of Lord Nelson's Life

1758	Sept. 29	Born at Burnham Thorpe, Norfolk, England.
1767	Dec. 26	Mother died.
1771	March	Entered the Navy at the age of 12. Went to sea in HMS *Raisonnable.*
	June	Voyage to West Indies in a merchant ship.
1772	July	Midshipman in HMS *Triumph.*
1773	June to October	Served on North Pole Expedition in HMS *Carcass.*
1773 to 1776	Oct. to March	Served on East India Station in HMS *Seahorse.*
1776	March	Embarked in HMS *Dolphin* for return to England on sick leave.
	Sept.	Arrived in England.
	Sept. 26	Ordered to HMS *Worcester* as acting Lieutenant, on convoy duty between England and Gibraltar.
1777	Apr. 8	Passed examination for Lieutenant.
	Apr. 10	Appointed Lieutenant of HMS *Lowestoffe.* Sailed to West Indies.
1778	July	Appointed Third Lieutenant of flagship HMS *Bristol.*

	Sept. 4	Appointed First Lieutenant of HMS *Bristol.*
	Dec. 8	Promoted to Commander and assigned to Brig HMS *Badger.*
1779	June	Spain joined the war against England.
	June 11	Promoted to Post Captain in command of HMS *Hinchinbrooke.*
1780	Jan. to April	Expedition up the San Juan River.
	May 2	Appointed Captain of HMS *Janus.*
	Aug. 30	Malaria forced him to resign command of HMS *Janus.*
		Sailed from Jamaica to England in HMS *Lion.*
	Nov.	Arrived at Spithead and went to Bath.
1781	Aug.	Appointed Captain of HMS *Albemarle.*
	Oct.	Convoy duty in North Sea.
1782	Jan.	HMS *Albemarle* under repair at Portsmouth.
	Apr. 17	Sailed in HMS *Albemarle* to Quebec, Canada.
	May 27	Arrived at Newfoundland.
	July 1	Arrived at Quebec.
	Aug. 14	Chased by French men-of-war near Boston.
	Sept. 17	Returned to Quebec.
	Oct.	Sailed with a convoy to New York.
	Nov. 11	Arrived in New York.
	Dec.	Sailed to the West Indies.
1783	Jan.	Great Britain made peace with Spain and America.
	May	Sailed for England.
	June 25	Arrived at Spithead.
	July 3	HMS *Albemarle* was "paid off."
		Returned to Burnham Thorpe.
	Oct.	Visited France during peacetime.

1784	Jan. 17	Returned to England from France.
	Mar. 18	Appointed Captain of HMS *Boreas*.
	May	Sailed to the West Indies.
	June 26	Arrived at Barbados.
1784–1787		Stopped the illegal trade in Leeward Islands, W.I.
1787	Mar. 11	Married Frances Nisbet.
	June 7	Sailed for England.
	July 4	HMS *Boreas* arrived at Spithead.
	Nov. 30	HMS *Boreas* was "paid off."
1787–1793		Nelson lived ashore with his family for five years at Burnham Thorpe.
1789	—	Outbreak of the French Revolution.
1792	—	France declared war on Austria.
1793	Jan. 30	Appointed Captain of HMS *Agamemnon.*
	Feb. 2	France declared war on Great Britain and Holland.
	May 23	Joined Lord Hood's Fleet and sailed for the Mediterranean.
	July 14	Blockade of Toulon, France, began.
	Aug. 27	Toulon occupied by the British.
	Sept. 11	Arrived at Naples, Italy, to request troops for the defense of Toulon against Napoleon's forces.
	Oct. 5	Rejoined Fleet at Toulon.
	Oct. 22	Engaged the French frigate *Melpomene* off Sardinia.
	Oct. 24	At Cagliari, Island of Sardinia.
	Nov.	Tunis Bay, North Africa.
	Dec. 19	Toulon in hands of French revolutionary forces.
1794	Feb.	San Fiorenzo, Corsica.
	Apr. 4	Siege of Bastia on Island of Corsica.
	May 22	Bastia surrendered.
	June 18	Landed for Siege of Calvi.
	July 12	Wounded and lost sight of right eye.

	Aug. 10	Calvi surrendered.
	Oct.	Cruising off Toulon and Corsica.
	Nov.	HMS *Agamemnon* refitting at Leghorn.
1795	Jan.	HMS *Agamemnon* joined Admiral Hotham's Fleet in the Mediterranean.
	Mar. 13–14	Engaged *Ca Ira* with the French Fleet.
	July 4	Sailed with small squadron to assist General de Vins on Italian Riviera.
	July 13	Action with French Fleet.
	July	Operations on Italian Riviera.
	Nov. 29	Sir John Jervis took command of Mediterranean Fleet.
	Dec.	HMS *Agamemnon* at Leghorn.
1796	—	French armies under Napoleon invade Italy. Spain declared war on England and the British Fleet was ordered to retreat from the Mediterranean.
	Jan.	HMS *Agamemnon* joined Fleet in San Fiorenzo Bay.
	Apr. 4	Hoisted Commodore's pennant in HMS *Agamemnon.*
	June 11	Shifted pennant to HMS *Captain.*
	Oct.	Evacuation of British from Bastia.
	Dec. 10	Shifted pennant to HMS *Minerve.*
	Dec. 20	Engaged Spanish frigate *La Sabina.*
	Dec. 26	Arrived to evacuate British forces on Elba.
1797	Feb. 11	Sailed in HMS *Minerve* from Gibraltar.
	Feb. 13	Again hoisted pennant in HMS *Captain.*
	Feb. 14	Battle of Cape St. Vincent. Temporarily shifted pennant to HMS *Irresistible.*
	Feb. 20	Promoted to Rear Admiral of the Blue.
	Mar. 17	Became Knight of the Bath.
	Mar. 24	Shifted pennant back to HMS *Captain.*
	Apr. 1	Hoisted Admiral's flag in HMS *Captain,* upon hearing of his promotion.

	Apr. 12	Escorted army troop ships from Elba to Gibraltar.
	May 27	Shifted flag to HMS *Theseus.*
	June	Commanded inshore blockade off Cádiz.
	July 15	Sailed for Canary Islands.
	July 24	Lost right arm in unsuccessful attack on Teneriffe, Santa Cruz Island.
	Aug. 20	Shifted flag to HMS *Seahorse* and sailed for England.
	Sept. 1	Arrived at Spithead.
	Sept. 27	Invested as Knight of the Bath.
1798	Mar. 29	Hoisted his flag in HMS *Vanguard.*
	Apr. 30	Joined St. Vincent's Fleet off Cádiz, and sailed in search of French Fleet.
	June 17	Off Naples.
	June 26	Alexandria.
	July 19	Syracuse.
	Aug. 1	Victory at the Battle of the Nile.
	Aug. 19	Sailed for Naples in HMS *Vanguard.*
	Sept. 22	Welcomed at Naples.
	Nov.	Attack on French at Rome and Leghorn.
	Nov. 6	Created Baron Nelson of the Nile and Burnham Thorpe.
	Dec. 23	Sailed for Palermo with Royal Family and Hamiltons.
	Dec. 26	Arrived at Palermo.
1799	Feb. 14	Promoted to Rear Admiral of the Red.
	June 8	Shifted his flag to HMS *Foudroyant.*
	June 24	Arrived off Naples.
	Aug. 8	Returned to Palermo.
	Aug. 13	Created Duke of Brontë.
1800	Feb. 18	Capture of *Le Genereux.*
	Mar. 30	Capture of *Le Guillaume Tell.*
	July 14	Struck his flag at Leghorn, and returned to England with the Hamiltons.
	Nov. 6	Arrived at Yarmouth.

	Nov. 20	Took his seat in the House of Lords.
1801	Jan. 1	Promoted to Vice Admiral of the Blue.
	Jan. 17	Hoisted flag in HMS *San Josef*.
	Jan. 30	Daughter Horatia born.
	Feb.12	Shifted flag to HMS *St. George*.
	Mar. 12	Sailed from Yarmouth for the Baltic.
	Mar. 26	Shifted flag to HMS *Elephant*.
	Apr. 2	Battle of Copenhagen. Shifted flag back to HMS *St. George*.
	Apr. 21	Appointed Commander-in-chief in the Baltic.
	May	Sailed to Russia.
	May 22	Created Viscount Nelson of the Nile and of Burnham Thorpe.
	June 19	Relieved of command in the Baltic and sailed for England.
	July 1	Arrived at Yarmouth.
	July 24	Appointed Commander-in-chief of Channel Squadron to prevent French invasion.
	July 27	Hoisted flag in *L'Unite*, and later sailed in HMS *Medusa* and HMS *Amazon*.
	Aug. 16	British attack on Boulogne flotilla.
1802	Mar. 25	Treaty of Amiens signed. Peace between Britain and France.
	Apr. 10	Struck his flag and left for Merton.
1803	May 16	Appointed Commander-in-chief in the Mediterranean.
	May 18	Britain declared war on France.
	May 18	Hoisted flag in HMS *Victory* at Spithead and sailed two days later.
	May 21	Shifted flag to HMS *Amphion*.
	July 8	Joined fleet off Toulon.
	July 30	Returned to HMS *Victory* and blockaded Toulon until April, 1805.
1804	Apr. 23	Promoted to Vice Admiral of the White.

	Dec.	Spain joined France and declared war on England.
1805	Jan. 17	French Fleet put to sea from Toulon, but returned to port. Nelson's search for the French Fleet began.
	Mar. 30	French Fleet again put to sea. Search resumed.
	May 11	Sailed for West Indies.
	June 4	Arrived at Barbados.
	June 6–7	Off Tobago and Trinidad. Enemy fleet sailed for France.
	June 13	Sailed from Antigua back to Europe.
	July 19	Anchored at Gibraltar.
	Aug. 15	Joined Cornwallis off Brest.
	Aug. 18	Arrived at Spithead and went to Merton.
	Sept. 2	Blackwood arrived with news that French Fleet had put into Cádiz.
	Sept. 13	Left Merton for Spithead.
	Sept. 14	Rehoisted flag in HMS *Victory* at Portsmouth.
	Sept. 15	Sailed from Spithead.
	Sept. 28	Joined Fleet off Cádiz.
	Oct. 19–20	French and Spanish combined fleets sailed out of Cádiz.
	Oct. 21	Nelson is killed at the Battle of Trafalgar.
1806	Jan. 9	Buried in St. Paul's Cathedral in London.

INDEX

INDEX

O

P

Q

R

S

T